CONTENTS

ARTIFICIAL INTELLIGENCE

by R Pon Mahesh

COPYRIGHT PAGE

DEDICATION PAGE

This book is dedicated to my father, mother & brother. Thanks for always being there for me.

PREFACE

Hi, this is Pon Mahesh, and I welcome you to this session on Artificial Intelligence full course. In this book, I'll be covering all the domains and the concepts involved under the umbrella of artificial intelligence, and I will also be showing you a couple of use cases and practical implementations by using Python. So, there's a lot to cover in this session, and let me quickly run you through agenda.

Note :

I gave some important links at the end of the book, please refer that to get detailed information. And i add some images for that pratical demos.

AGENDA

So, we're gonna begin the session by understanding the history of artificial intelligence and how it came into existence. We'll follow this by looking at why we're talking about artificial intelligence now, why has it gotten so famous right now. Then we'll look at what exactly is artificial intelligence. We'll discuss the applications of artificial intelligence, after which we'll discuss the basics of AI where in we'll understand the different types of artificial intelligence.

We'll follow this by understanding the different programming languages that can be used to study AI. And we'll understand why we're gonna choose Python. Alright, I'll introduce you to Python. And then we'll move on and discuss machine learning. Here we'll discuss the different types of machine learning, the different algorithms involved in machine learning, which include classification algorithms, regression algorithms, clustering, and association algorithms.

To make you understand machine learning better, we'll run a couple of demos wherein we'll see how machine learning algorithms are used to solve real world problems. After that, we'll discuss the limitations of machine learning and why deep learning is needed. I'll introduce you to the deep learning concept, what are neurons, perceptron's, multiple layer perceptron's and so on.

We'll discuss the different types of neural networks, and we'll also look at what exactly back propagation is. Apart from this, we'll be running a demo to understand deep learning in more depth. And finally, we'll move onto the next module, which is natural language processing.

On the natural language processing, we'll try to understand what is text mining, the difference between text mining in NLP, what are the different terminologies in NLP, and we'll end the session by looking at the practical implementation of NLP using Python, alright.

So, guys, there's a lot to cover in today's session. Also, if you want to stay updated about the recent technologies, and would like to learn more about the training technology, we will give some links in the end of the book for demo purpose and you are updated in future.

INTRODUCTION

Artificial intelligence the next big thing but why do we need . I hear a lot lying in his grade let's go back into time and see what happened with an example

Alan met with a major accident because of driving back home trunk along with 10,000. 265 other people the same every year this number is increasing and we have cars that can drive on its own that can save people like Alan Jack is blind he wishes for a device that could help him to see the world meet Olivia she is visiting Berlin she cannot understand German sign words.

she wishes for a software that can convert those German words in English looking at all the scenarios what do we understand we need an intelligent machine which has the power to think analyse and make decisions this is nothing but artificial intelligence the basic idea is to mimic a human brain inside a machine for example if we want a car to drive on its own we need to train that car based on drivers experience with the AI people like Alan can sit comfortably in self-driving car and reach home safely you will be amazed to know that.
bondsman's that have been made in this field AI has also held people like Jack or camps my eye is a small wearable device that has the ability to read printed text from any surface the device also recognizes faces at individuals as well as identifies products denominations of currency notes

Fortunately we have AI enabled mobile apps that can extract the text from an image and converted into a different language artificial intelligence is not only saving our lives or making it comfortable.

But it is also contributing in the field of art meet Eric the famous painter which has a computer program Aaron is able to create very unique and exquisite paintings as software's are even composing music ai has given us word script which can create a unique story for you it writes articles in newspapers and on internet we even have Sherlock and intelligent tutoring system teaching air force technicians how to diagnose electrical problems and aircrafts so clearly after internet which is connect as the entire world and microchips without which more than humans cannot survive AI is the next big thing.

That is revolutionising the world the question is what are the technologies that are driving this advancements in the field of AI first game machine learning for achieving AI and now people are talking about deep learning which is a subfield machine learning deep learning works in the same way how a human brain works it is inspired from neem logs which are nothing but brain cells deep learning uses multiple artificial human.

These neurons are arranged in the form of layers output of every layer is the input to the next layer earlier due to less data and lack of computation of power deep learning was not possible but now we have GPUs a huge amount of data because of which deep learning models give very high accuracy for deep learning the most famous programming language is pipeline and tensor flow is a Python package for implementing deep learning products.

so read and master the concepts of AI and deep learning with Artificial Intelligence structured program which includes neural networks convolutional neural networks recurrent neural networks RBM and autoencoders using sensor flow.

WHAT IS ARTIFICIAL INTELLIGENCE?

The concept of artificial intelligence goes back to the classical ages. Under Greek mythology, the concept of machines and mechanical men were well thought of. So, an example of this is Talos. I don't know how many of you have heard of this. Talos was a giant animated bronze warrior who was programmed to guard the island of Crete.

Now these are just ideas. Nobody knows if this was actually implemented, but machine learning and AI were thought of long ago. Now let's get back to the 19th century. Now 1950 was speculated to be one of the most important years for the introduction of artificial intelligence. In 1950, Alan Turing published a paper in which he speculated about the possibility of creating machines that think.

So, he created what is known as the Turing test. This test is basically used to determine whether or not a computer can think intelligently like a human being. He noted that thinking is difficult to define and devised his famous Turing test.

2011 – IBM Watson

IBM's question answering system, *Watson*, defeated the two greatest Jeopardy! champions, Brad Rutter and Ken Jennings,.

So, basically, if a machine can carry out a conversation that was indistinguishable from a conversation with a human being, it was reasonable to say that the machine is thinking, meaning that the machine will pass the Turing test. Now, unfortunately, up to this date, we haven't found a machine that has fully cleared the Turing test.

So, the Turing test was actually the first serious proposal in the philosophy of artificial intelligence. Followed by this was the era of 1951. This was also known as the game AI. So, in 1951, by using the Ferranti Mark 1 machine of the University of Manchester, a computer scientist known as Christopher Strachey wrote a checkers program.

And at the same time, a program was written for chess as well. Now, these programs were later improved and redone, but this was the first attempt at creating programs that could play chess or that would compete with humans in playing chess.

This is followed by the year 1956. Now, this is probably the most important year in the invention of AI. Because in 1956, for the first time, the was coined. Alright. So, the term artificial intelligence was coined by John McCarthy at the Dartmouth Conference in 1956. Coming to the year 1959, the first AI laboratory was established.

This period marked the research era for AI. So, the first AI lab where research was performed is the MIT lab, which is still running till date. In 1960, the first robot was introduced to the General Motors assembly line. In 1961, the first chatbot was invented. Now we have Siri, we have Alexa. But in 1961, there was a chatbot known as Eliza, which was introduced.

This is followed by the famous IBM Deep Blue. In 1997, the news broke down that IBM's Deep Blue beats the world champion, Garry Kasparov, in the game of chess. So, this was kind of the first accomplishment of AI. It was able to beat the world champion at chess.

So, in 2005, when the DARPA Grand Challenge was held, a robotic car named Stanley, which was built by Stanford's racing team, won the DARPA Grand Challenge. That was another big accomplish of AI. In 2011, IBM's question answering system, Watson, defeated the two greatest Jeopardy champions, Brad Rutter and Ken Jennings.

So, guys, this was how AI evolved. It started off as a hypothetical situation. Right now, it's the most important technology in today's world. If you look around everywhere, everything around us is run through AI deep learning or machine learning. So, since the emergence of AI in the 1950s, we have actually seen an exponential growth and its potential.

So, AI covers domains such as machine learning, deep learning, neural networks, natural language processing, knowledge based, expert systems and so on. It is also made its way into computer vision and image processing.

Now the question here is if AI has been here for over half a century, why has it suddenly gained so much importance? Why are we talking about artificial intelligence now?

DEMAND FOR AI

Let me tell you the main reasons for the demand of AI. The first reason is what we have more computation power now. So, artificial intelligence requires a lot of computing power. Recently, many advances have been made and complex deep learning models are deployed. And one of the greatest technologies that made this possible are GPUs.

Since we have more computational power now, it is possible for us to implement AI in our daily aspects. Second most important reason is that we have a lot of data at present. We're generating data at an immeasurable pace. We are generating data through social media, through IoT devices. Every possible way, there's a lot of data.

So, we need to find a method or a solution that can help us process this much data, and help us derive useful insight, so that we can grow business with the help of data. Alright, so, that process is basically artificial intelligence.

So, in order to have a useful AI agent to make smart decisions like telling which item to recommend next when you shop online, or how to classify an object from an image. AI are trained on large data sets, and big data enables us to do this more efficiently. Next reason is now we have better algorithms.

DEMAND FOR AI

More Computational Power · More Data · Better algorithms · Broad Investment

Right now, we have very effective algorithms which are based on the idea of neural networks. Neural networks are nothing but the concept behind deep learning. Since we have better algorithms which can do better computations and quicker computations with more accuracy, the demand for AI has increased.

Another reason is that universities, governments, startup, and tech giants are all investing in AI. Okay, so companies like Google, Amazon, Facebook, Microsoft, all of these companies have heavily invested in artificial intelligence because they believe that AI is the future. So, AI is rapidly growing both as a field of study and also as an economy.

So, actually, this is the right time for you to understand what is AI and how it works. So, let's move on and understand what exactly artificial intelligence is.

ARTIFICIAL INTELLIGENCE

The term artificial intelligence was first coined in the year 1956 by John McCarthy at the Dartmouth Conference. I already mentioned this before. It was the birth of AI in the 1956. Now, how did he define artificial intelligence? John McCarthy defined AI as the science and engineering of making intelligent machines.

In other words, artificial intelligence is the theory and development of computer systems able to perform task that normally require human intelligence, such as visual perception, speech recognition, decision making, and translation between languages. So, guys, in a sense, AI is a technique of getting machines to work and behave like humans.

In the rest past, artificial intelligence has been able to accomplish this by creating machines and robots that have been used in wide range of fields, including healthcare, robotics, marketing, business analytics, and many more. With this in mind, let's discuss a couple of real-world application of AI, so that you understand how important artificial intelligence is in today's world.

John McCarthy first coined the term Artificial Intelligence in the year 1956.

John McCarthy defined Artificial Intelligence as the science and engineering of making intelligent machines.

AI APPLICATIONS

Now, one of the most famous applications of artificial intelligence is the Google predictive search engine. When you begin typing a search term and Google makes recommendations for you to choose from, that is artificial intelligence in action.

So predictive searches are based on data that Google collects about you, such as your browser history, your location, your age, and other personal details. So by using artificial intelligence, Google attempts to guess what you might be trying to find. Now behind this, there's a lot of natural language processing, deep learning, and machine learning involved. We'll be discussing all of those concepts in the further slides.

It's not very simple to create a search engine, but the logic behind Google search engine is artificial intelligence. Moving on, in the finance sector, JP Morgan Chase's Contract Intelligence Platform uses machine learning, artificial intelligence, and image recognition software to analyse legal documents.

Now let me tell you that manually reviewing around 12,000 agreements took over 36,000 hours. That's a lot of time. But as soon as this task was replaced by AI machine, it was able to do this in a matter of seconds. So that's the difference between artificial intelligence and manual or human work. Even though AI cannot think and reason like humans, but their computational power is very strong compared to humans, because the machine learning algorithm, deep learning concepts, and natural language processing, AI has reached a stage wherein it can compute the most complex of complex problems in a matter of seconds.

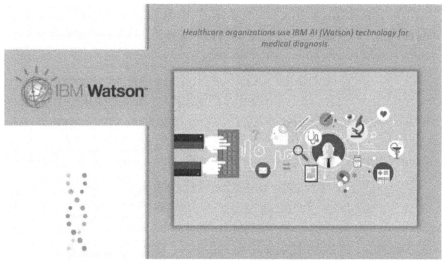

Healthcare organizations use IBM AI (Watson) technology for medical diagnosis.

Coming to healthcare, IBM is one of the pioneers that has developed AI software, specifically for medicine. Let me tell you that more than 230 healthcare organizations use IBM AI technology, which is basically IBM Watson. In 2016, IBM Watson technology was able to cross reference 20 million oncology records quickly and correctly diagnose a rare leukemic condition in a patient.

So, it basically went through 20 million records, which it probably did in a matter of second or minutes, max to max. And then it correctly diagnosed a patient with a rare leukemic. Knowing that machines are now used in medical fields as well, it shows how important AI has become. It has reached every domains of our lives. Let me give you another example. The Google's AI Eye Doctor is another initiative, which is taken by Google, where they're working with an Indian eye care chain to develop artificial intelligence system which can examine retinal scans and identify a condition called diabetic retinopathy which can cause blindness.

Now in social media platforms like Facebook, artificial intelligence is used for face verification wherein you make use of machine learning and deep learning concept in order to detect facial features and tag your friends. All the auto tagging feature that you see in Facebook, behind that there's machine learning, deep learning, neural networks. There's only AI behind it.

So we're actually unaware that we use AI very regularly in our life. All the social media platforms like Instagram, Facebook, Twitter, they heavily rely on artificial intelligence. Another such example is Twitter's AI which is being used to identify any sort of hate speech and terroristic languages in tweets.

So again, it makes use of machine leaning, deep learning, natural language processing in order to filter out any offensive or any reportable content. Now recently, the company discovered around 300,000 terroristic link accounts and 95% of these were found by non-human artificially intelligent machines.

Coming to virtual assistants, we have virtual assistants like Siri and Alexa right now. Let me tell you about another newly released Google's virtual assistant called the Google Duplex, which has astonished millions of people around the world. Not only can it respond to calls and book appointments for you, it also adds a human touch.

So it adds human filters and all of that. It makes it sound very realistic. It's actually very hard to distinguish between human and the AI speaking over the phone. Another famous application is AI is self-driving cars.

So, artificial intelligence implements computer vision, image detection, deep learning, in order to build cars that can automatically detect any objects or any obstacles and drive around without human intervention.

So these are fully automated self-driving cars. Also, Elon Musk talks a lot about how AI is implemented in Tesla's self-driving cars. He quoted that Tesla will have fully self-driving cars ready by the end of the year, and robo taxi version that can ferry passengers without anyone behind the wheel.

So if you look at it, AI is actually used by the tech giants. A lot of tech giant companies like Google, Tesla, Facebook, all of these data-driven companies. In fact, Netflix also makes use of AI,. So, coming to Netflix.

So with the help of artificial intelligence and machine learning, Netflix has developed a personalized movie recommendation for each of its users. So if each of you opened up Netflix and if you look at the type of movies that are recommended to you, they are different. This is because Netflix studies each user's personal details, and tries to understand what each user is interested in and what sort of movie patterns each user has, and then it recommends movies to them.

So Netflix uses the watching history of other users with similar taste to recommend what you may be most interested in watching next, so that you can stay engaged and continue your monthly subscription. Also, there's a known fact that over 75% of what you watch is recommended by Netflix. So their recommendation engine is brilliant.

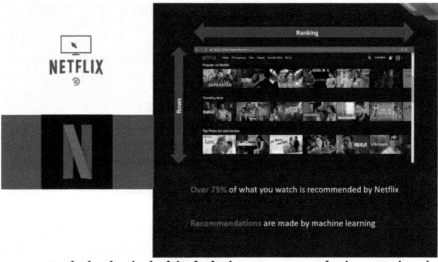

And the logic behind their recommendation engine is machine learning and artificial intelligence. Apart from Netflix, Gmail also uses AI on an everyday basis. If you open up your inbox right now, you will notice that there are separate sections. For example, we have primary section, social section, and all of that. Gmail has a separate section called the spam mails also.

So, what Gmail does is it makes use of concepts of artificial intelligence and machine learning algorithms to classify emails as spam and non-spam. Many times, certain words or phrases are frequently used in spam emails. If notice your spam emails, they have words like lottery, earn, full refund. All of this denotes that the email is more likely to be a spam one.

So, such words and correlations are understood by using machine learning and natural language processing and a few other aspects of artificial intelligence. So, guys, these were the common applications of artificial intelligence. Now let's discuss the different types of AI.

TYPES OF AI

AI is divided into three different evolutionary stages, or you can say that there are three stages of artificial intelligence. Of course, we have artificial narrow intelligence followed by artificial general intelligence, and that is followed by artificial super intelligence.

Artificial narrow intelligence, which is also known as weak AI, it involves applying artificial intelligence only to specific task. So, many currently existing systems that claim to use artificial intelligence are actually operating as weak AI focused on a narrowly defined specific problem Let me give you an example of artificial narrow intelligence. Alexa is a very good example of weak AI.

It operates within unlimited pre-defined range of functions. There's no genuine intelligence or there is no self-awareness, despite being a sophisticated example of weak AI. The Google search engine, Sophia the humanoid, self-driving cars, and even the famous AlphaGo fall under the category of weak AI.

So, guys, right now we're at the stage of artificial narrow intelligence or weak AI. We actually haven't reached artificial general intelligence or artificial super intelligence, but let's look at what exactly it would be like if we reach artificial general intelligence.

Now artificial general intelligence which is also known as strong AI, it involves machines that possess the ability to perform any intelligent task that a human being can. Now this is actually something that a lot of people don't realize. Machines don't possess human-like abilities.

They have a very strong processing unit that can perform high-level computations, but they're not yet capable of doing the simple and the most reasonable things that a human being can. If you tell a machine to process like a million documents, it'll probably do that in a matter of 10 seconds, or a minute, or even 10 minutes.

But if you ask a machine to walk up to your living room and switch on the TV, a machine will take forever to learn that, because machines don't have the reasonable way of thinking. They have a very strong processing unit, but they're not yet capable of thinking and reasoning like a human being. So that's exactly why we're still stuck on artificial narrow intelligence.

So far, we haven't developed any machine that can fully be called strong AI, even though there are examples of AlphaGo Zero which defeated AlphaGo in the game of Go. AlphaGo Zero basically learned in a span of four months.

It learned on its own without any human intervention. But even then, it was not classified as a fully strong artificial intelligence, because it cannot reason like a human being. Moving onto artificial super intelligence. Now this is a term referring to the time when the capabilities of a computer will surpass that of a human being.

In all actuality, I'll take a while for us to achieve artificial super intelligence. Presently, it's seen as a hypothetical situation as depicted in movies and any science fiction books wherein machines have taken over the world, movies like Terminator and all of that depict artificial super intelligence.

These don't exist yet, which we should be thankful for, but there are a lot of people who speculate that artificial super intelligence will take over the world by the year 2040. So, guys, these were the different types or different stages of artificial intelligence. To summarize everything, like I said before, narrow intelligence is the only thing that exist for now. We have only weak AI or weak artificial intelligence.

PROGRAMMING LANGUAGES FOR AI

PROGRAMMING LANGUAGES FOR AI

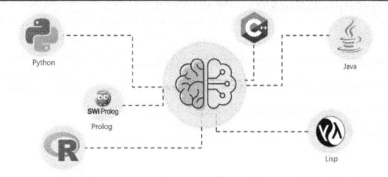

All the major AI technologies that you see are artificial narrow intelligence. We don't have any machines which are capable of thinking like human beings or reasoning like a human being. Now let's move on and discuss the different programming language for AI.

So, there are actually N number of languages that can be used for artificial intelligence. I'm gonna mention a few of them. So, first, we have Python. Python is probably the most famous language for artificial intelligence. It's also known as the most effective language for AI, because a lot of developers prefer to use Python.

And a lot of scientists are also comfortable with the Python language. This is partly because the syntaxes which belong to Python are very simple and they can be learned very easily. It's considered to be one of the easiest languages to learn. And also, many other AI algorithms and machine learning algorithms can be easily implemented in Python, because there are a lot of libraries which are predefined functions for these algorithms.

So, all you have to do is you have to call that function. You don't actually have to call your algorithm. So, Python is considered the best choice for artificial intelligence. With Python stands R, which is a statistical programming language.

Now R is one of the most effective language and environment for analysing and manipulating the data for statistical purpose. It is a statistical programming language. So, using R we can easily produce well designed publication quality plots, including mathematical symbol and formula, wherever needed.

If you ask me, I think R is also one of the easiest programming languages to learn. The syntax is very similar to English language, and it also has N number of libraries that support statistics, data science, AI, machine learning, and so on. It also has predefined functions for machine learning algorithms, natural language processing, and so on.

So, R is also a very good choice if you want to get started with programming languages for machine learning or AI. Apart from this, we have Java. Now Java can also be considered as a good choice for AI development. Artificial intelligence has a lot to do with search algorithms, artificial neural networks, and genetic programming, and Java provides many benefits. It's easy to use. Debugging is very easy, package services.

There is simplified work with large scale projects. There's a good user interaction, and graphical representation of data. It has something known as the standard widget toolkit, which can be used for making graphs and interfaces. So, graphic virtualization is actually a very important part of AI, or data science, or machine learning for that matter.

Let me list out a few more languages. We also have something known as Lisp. Now shockingly, a lot of people have not heard of this language. This is actually the oldest and the most suited language for the development of artificial intelligence. It is considered to be a language which is very suited for the development of artificial intelligence.

Now let me tell you that this language was invented by John McCarthy who's also known as the father of artificial intelligence. He was the person who coined the term artificial intelligence. It has the capability of processing symbolic information.

It has excellent prototyping capabilities. It is easy, and it creates dynamic objects with a lot of ease. There's automatic garbage collection in all of that. But over the years, because of advancements, many of these features have migrated into many other languages. And that's why a lot of people don't go for Lisp.

There are a lot of new languages which have more effective features or which have better packages you can see. Another language I like to talk about is Prologue. Prologue is frequently used in knowledge base and expert systems. The features provided by Prologue include pattern matching, freebase data structuring, automatic back tracking and so on.

All of these features provide a very powerful and flexible programming framework. Prologue is actually widely used in medical projects and also for designing expert AI systems. Apart from this, we also have C++, we have SaaS, we have JavaScript which can also be used for AI. We have MATLAB, we have Julia.

All of these languages are actually considered pretty good languages for artificial intelligence. But for now, if you ask me which programming language should I go for, I would say Python. Python has all the possible packages, and it is very easy to understand and easy to learn. So, let's look at a couple of features of Python.

We can see why we should go for Python. First of all, Python was created in the year 1989. It is actually a very easy programming language. That's one of the reasons why a lot of people prefer Python. It's very easy to understand. It's very easy to grasp this language.

So, Python is an interpreted, object-oriented, high-level programming language, and it can be very easily implemented. Now let me tell you a few features of Python. It's very simple and easy to learn. Like I mentioned, it is one of the easiest programming languages, and it also free and open source. Apart from that, it is a high-level language.

You don't have to worry about anything like memory allocation. It is portable, meaning that you can use it on any platform like Linux, Windows, Macintosh, Solaris, and so on. It supports different programming paradigms like object-oriented and procedure-oriented programming, and it is extensible, meaning that it can invoke C and C++ libraries.

Apart from this, let me tell you that Python is actually gaining unbelievable huge momentum in AI. The language is used to develop data science algorithms, machine learning algorithms, and IoT projects. The other advantages to Python also, the fact that you don't have to code much when it comes to Python for AI or machine learning. This is because there are ready-made packages.

There are predefined packages that have all the function and algorithm stored. For example, there is something known as PiBrain, which can be used for machine learning, NumPy which can be used for scientific computation, Pandas and so on.

There are N number of libraries in Python. So guys, I'm now going to go into depth of Python. I'm now going to explain Python to you, since this session is about artificial intelligence. So, those of you who don't know much about Python or who are new to Python, I will leave a couple of links in the description box.

You all can get started with programming and any other concepts or any other doubts that you have on Python. We have a lot of content around programming with Python or Python for machine learning and so on. Now let's move on and talk about one of the most important aspects of artificial intelligence,

INTRODUCTION TO MACHINE LEARNING

which is machine learning. Now a lot of people always ask me this question. Is machine learning and artificial intelligence the same thing? Well, both of them are not the same thing. The difference between AI and machine learning is that machine learning is used in artificial intelligence.

Machine learning is a method through which you can feed a lot of data to a machine and make it learn. Now AI is a vast of field. Under AI, we have machine learning, we have NLP, we have expert systems, we have image recognition, object detection, and so on. We have deep learning also.

So, AI is sort of a process or it's a methodology in which you make machines mimic the behaviour of human beings. Machine learning is a way in which you feed a lot of data to a machine, so that it can make it's own decisions. Let's get into depth about machine learning.

NEED FOR MACHINE LEARNING

So first, we'll understand the need for machine learning or why machine learning came into existence. Now the need for machine learning begins since the technical revolution itself. So, guys, since technology became the centre of everything, we've been generating an immeasurable amount of data.

NEED FOR MACHINE LEARNING

Cloud Data

Internet Of Things

Social Media

"Over 2.5 quintillion bytes of data are created every single day, and it's only going to grow from there. By 2020, it's estimated that 1.7MB of data will be created every second for every person on earth."

As per research, we generate around 2.5 quintillion bytes of data every single data every single day. And it is estimated that by this year, 2020, 1.7 mb of data will be created every second for every person on earth. For e.g.: - I'm speaking to you right now via YouTube, I'm generating a lot of data. Now you're watching this video on YouTube also accounts for data generation. **So, there's data everywhere**.

So, with the availability of so much data, it is finally possible to build predictive models that can study and analyse complex data to find useful insights and deliver more accurate results. So, top tier companies like Netflix and Amazon build such machine learning models by using tons of data in order to identify any profitable opportunity and avoid any unwanted risk.

So, guys, one thing you all need to know is that the most important thing for artificial intelligence is data. For artificial intelligence or whether it's machine learning or deep learning, it's always data. And now that we have a lot of data, we can find a way to analyse, process, and draw useful insights from this data in order to help us grow businesses or to find solutions to some problems.

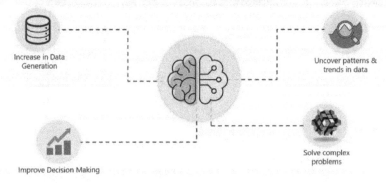

Data is the solution. We just need to know how to handle the data. And the way to handle data is through machine learning, deep learning, and artificial intelligence. A few reasons why machine learning is so important is, number one, due to increase in data generation. So due to excessive production of data, we need to find a method that can be used to structure, analyse, and draw useful insights from data, this is where machine learning comes in.

It is used to solve problems and find solutions through the most complex task faced by organizations. Apart from this, we also needed to improve decision making. So, by making use of various algorithms, machine learning can be used to make better business decisions. For example, machine learning is used to focus sales. It is used to predict any downfalls n the stock market or identify any sort of risk and anomalies. Other reasons include that machine learning helps us uncover patterns and trends in data.

So, finding hidden patterns and extracting key insights from data is the most important part of machine learning. So, by building predictive models and using statistical techniques, machine learning allows you to dig beneath the surface and explode the data at a minute scale. Understanding data and extracting patterns manually takes a lot of time. It'll take several days for us to extract any useful information from data.

But if you use machine learning algorithms, you can perform similar computations in less than a second. Another reason is we need to solve complex problems. So from detecting the genes linked to the deadly ALS disease, to building self-driving cars, machine learning can be used to solve the most complex problems.

At present, we also found a way to spot stars which are 2,400 light years away from our planet. Okay, all of this is possible through AI, machine learning, deep learning, and these techniques.

So to sum it up, machine learning is very important at present because we're facing a lot of issues with data. We're generating a lot of data, and we have to handle this data in such a way that in benefits us. So that's why machine learning comes in.

WHAT IS MACHINE LEARNING?

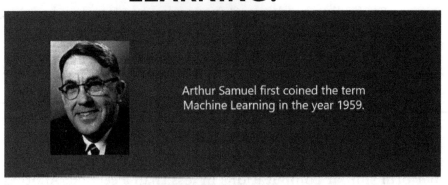

Arthur Samuel first coined the term Machine Learning in the year 1959.

What Is Machine Learning?

"A computer program is said to learn from experience E with respect to some class of tasks T and performance measure P if its performance at tasks in T, as measured by P, improves with experience E."

let me give you a short history of machine learning. So, machine learning was first coined by Arthur Samuel in the year 1959, which is just three years from when artificial intelligence was coined. So, looking back, that year was probably the most significant in terms of technological advancement, because most of the technologies today are based on the concept of machine learning.

Most of the AI technologies itself are based on the concept of machine learning and deep learning. Don't get confused about machine learning and deep learning. We'll discuss about deep learning in the further slides, where we'll also see the difference between AI, machine learning, and deep learning.

So coming back to what exactly machine learning is, if we browse through the internet, you'll find a lot of definitions about what exactly machine learning is. One of the definitions I found was a computer program is said to learn from experience

E with respect to some class of task T and performance measure P if its performance at task in T, as measured by P, improves with experience E. That's very confusing, so let me just narrow it down to you.

In simple terms, machine learning is a subset of artificial intelligence which provides machines the ability to learn automatically and improve with experience without being explicitly programmed to do so. In the sense, it is the practice of getting machines to solve problems by gaining the ability to think.

But now you might be thinking how can a machine think or make decisions. Now machines are very similar to humans. Okay, if you feed a machine a good amount of data, it will learn how to interpret, process, and analyse this data by using machine learning algorithms, and it will help you solve world problems.

So, what happens here is a lot of data is fed to the machine. The machine will train on this data and it'll build a predictive model with the help of machine learning algorithms in order to predict some outcome or in order to find some solution to a problem.

So, it involves data. You're gonna train the machine and build a model by using machine learning algorithms in order to predict some outcome or to find a solution to a problem. So that is a simple way of understanding what exactly machine learning is. I'll be going into more depth about machine learning, so don't worry if you have understood anything as of now. Now let's discuss a couple terms which are frequently used in machine learning.

MACHINE LEARNING DEFINITIONS

MACHINE LEARNING DEFINITIONS

Algorithm: *A set of rules and statistical techniques used to learn patterns from data*

Response Variable: *It is the feature or the output variable that needs to be predicted by using the predictor variable(s).*

Model: *A model is trained by using a Machine Learning Algorithm.*

Training Data: *The Machine Learning model is built using the training data.*

Predictor Variable: *It is a feature(s) of the data that can be used to predict the output.*

Testing Data: *The Machine Learning model is evaluated using the testing data.*

The first definition that we come across very often is an algorithm. So, basically, a machine learning algorithm is a set of rules and statistical techniques that is used to learn patterns from data and draw significant information from it. Okay. So, guys, the logic behind a machine learning model is basically the machine learning algorithm.

Okay, an example of a machine learning algorithm is linear regression, or decision tree, or a random forest. All of these are machine learning algorithms. We'll define the logic behind a machine learning model. Now what is a machine learning model?

A model is actually the main component of a machine learning process. Okay, so a model is trained by using the machine learning algorithm. The difference between an algorithm and a model is that an algorithm maps all the decisions that a model is supposed to take based on the given input in order to get the correct output.

So, the model will use the machine learning algorithm in order to draw useful insights from the input and give you an outcome that is very precise. That's the machine learning model. The next definition we have is predictor variable. Now a predictor variable is any feature of the data that can be used to predict the output.

Okay, let me give you an example to make you understand what a predictor variable is. Let's say you're trying to predict the height of a person, depending on his weight. So here your predictor variable becomes your weight, because you're using the weight of a person to predict the person's height.

So, your predictor variable becomes your weight. The next definition is response variable. Now in the same example, height would be the response variable. Response variable is also known as the target variable or the output variable. This is the variable that you're trying to predict by using the predictor variables.

So, a response variable is the feature or the output variable that needs to be predicted by using the predictor variables. Next, we have something known as training data. Now training and testing data are terminologies that you'll come across very often in a machine learning process. So, training data is basically the data that I used to create the machine learning model. So, basically in a machine learning process, when you feed data into the machine, it'll be divided into two parts.

So, splitting the data into two parts is also known as data splicing. So you'll take your input data, you'll divide it into two sections. One you'll call the training data, and the other you'll call the testing data.

So, then you have something known as the testing data. The training data is basically used to create the machine learning model. The training data helps the model to identify key trends and patterns which are essential to predict the output.

Now the testing data is, after the model is trained, it must be tested in order to evaluate how accurately it can predict an outcome. Now this is done by using the testing data. So, basically, the training data is used to train the model.

The testing data is used to test the efficiency of the model. Now let's move on and get our next topic, which is machine learning process. So, what is the machine learning process?

MACHINE LEARNING PROCESS

Now the machine learning process involves building a predictive model that can be used to find a solution for a problem statement. Now in order to solve any problem in machine learning, there are a couple of steps that you need to follow. Let's look at the steps.

The first step is you define the objective of your problem. And the second step is data gathering, which is followed by preparing your data, data exploration, building a model, model evaluation, and finally making predictions.

Now, in order to understand the machine learning process, let's assume that you've been given a problem that needs to be solved by using machine learning. So the problem that you need to solve is we need to predict the occurrence of rain in your local area by using machine learning. So, basically, you need to predict the possibility of rain by studying the weather conditions.

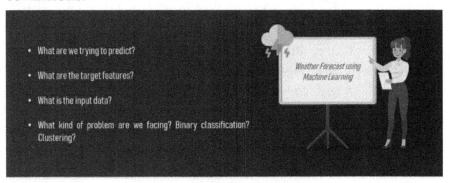

Step 1: Define the objective of the Problem
To predict the possibility of rain by studying the weather conditions.

So, what we did here is we basically looked at step number one, which is define the objective of the problem. Now here you need to answer questions such as what are we trying to predict. Is that output going to be a continuous variable, or is it going to be a discreet variable?

These are the kinds of questions that you need to answer in the first page, which is defining the objective of the problem, right? So yeah, exactly what are the target feature. So here you need to understand which is your target variable and what are the different predictor variables that you need in order to predict this outcome.

So here our target variable will be basically a variable that can tell us whether it's going to rain or not. Input data is we'll need data such as maybe the temperature on a particular day or the humidity level, the precipitation, and so on. So, you need to define the objective at this stage. So basically, you have to form an idea of the problem at this storage.

Another question that you need to ask yourself is what kind of problem are you solving. Is this a binary classification problem, or is this a clustering problem, or is this a regression problem? Now, a lot of you might not be familiar with the term's classification clustering and regression in terms of machine learning.

Don't worry, I'll explain all of these terms in the upcoming slides. All you need to understand at step one is you need to define how you're going to solve the problem. You need to understand what sort of data you need to solve the problem, how you're going to approach the problem, what are you trying to predict, what variables you'll need in order to predict the outcome, and so on.

Let's move on and look at step number two, which is data gather. Now in this stage, you must be asking questions such as, what kind of data is needed to solve this problem? And is this data available? And if it is available, from where can I get this data and how can I get the data? Data gathering is one of the most time-consuming steps in machine learning process.

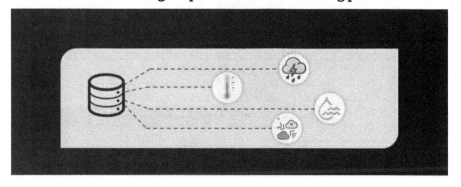

Step 2: Data Gathering

Data such as weather conditions, humidity level, temperature, pressure, etc are either collected manually or scarped from the web.

If you have to go manually and collect the data, it's going to take a lot of time. But lucky for us, there are a lot of resources online, which were wide data sets. All you need to do is web scraping where you just have to go ahead and download data. One of the websites I can tell you all about is Cargill.

So, if you're a beginner in machine learning, don't worry about data gathering and all of that. All you have to do is go to websites such as Cargill and just download the data set. So coming back to the problem that we are discussing, which is predicting the weather, the data needed for weather forecasting includes measures like humidity level, the temperature, the pressure, the locality, whether or not you live in a hill station, such data has to be collected or stored for analysis.

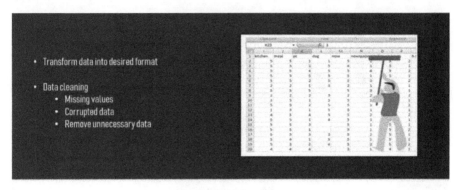

- Transform data into desired format

- Data cleaning
  - Missing values
  - Corrupted data
  - Remove unnecessary data

Step 3: Preparing Data

Data Cleaning involves getting rid of inconsistencies in data such as missing values or redundant variables.

So, all the data is collected during the data gathering stage. This step is followed by data preparation, or also known as data cleaning. So, if you're going around collecting data, it's almost never in the right format.

And even if you are taking data from online resources from any website, even then, the data will require cleaning and preparation. The data is never in the right format. You have to do some sort of preparation and some sort of cleaning in order to make the data ready for analysis.

So, what you'll encounter while cleaning data is, you'll encounter a lot of inconsistencies in the data set, like you'll encounter some missing values, redundant variables, duplicate values, and all of that. So, removing such inconsistencies is very important, because they might lead to any wrongful computations and predictions.

Okay, so at this stage you can scan the data set for any inconsistencies, and you can fix them then and there. Now let me give you a small fact about data cleaning. So there was a survey that was ran last year or so. I'm not sure. And a lot of data scientists were asked which step was the most difficult or the most annoying and time-consuming of all.

And 80% of the data scientist said it was data cleaning. Data cleaning takes up 80% of their time. So it's not very easy to get rid of missing values and corrupted data. And even if you get rid of missing values, sometimes your data set might get affected.

It might get biased because maybe one variable has too many missing values, and this will affect your outcome. So, you'll have to fix such issue, we'll have to deal with all of this missing data and corrupted data.

Step 4: Exploratory Data Analysis

Data Exploration involves understanding the patterns and trends in the data. At this stage all the useful insights are drawn and correlations between the variables are understood.

So, data cleaning is actually one of the hardest steps in machine learning process. Okay, now let's move on and look at our next step, which is exploratory data analysis. So here what you do is basically become a detective in the stage. So this stage, which is EDA or exploratory data analysis, is like the brainstorming stage of machine learning.

Data exploration involves understanding the patterns and the trends in your data. So, at this stage, all the useful insights are drawn and any correlations between the various variables are understood. What do I mean by trends and patterns and correlations? Now let's consider our example which is we have to predict the rainfall on a particular day.

So we know that there is a strong possibility of rain if the temperature has fallen law. So, we know that our output will depend on variables such as temperature, humidity, and so on. Now to what level it depends on these variables, we'll have to find out that. We'll have to find out the patterns, and we'll find out the correlations between such variables.

So, such patterns and trends have to be understood and mapped at this stage. So, this is what exploratory data analysis is about. It's the most important part of machine learning. This is where you'll understand what exactly your data is and how you can form the solution to your problem. The next step in a machine learning process is building a machine learning module.

All the insights and the patterns that you derive during the data exploration are used to build a machine learning model. So, this stage always begins by splitting the data set into two parts, which is training data and testing data. I've already discussed with you that the data that you used in a machine learning process is always split into two parts.

We have the training data and we have the testing data. Now when you're building a model, you always use the training data. So you always make use of the training data in order to build the model. Now a lot of you might be asking what is training data. Is it different from the input data that you're feeding with the machine or is it different from the testing data? Now training data is the same input data that you're feeding to the machine.

Step 5: Building a Machine Learning Model

At this stage a Predictive Model is built by using Machine Learning Algorithms such as Linear Regression, Decision Trees, etc.

The only difference is that you're splitting the data set

into two. You're randomly picking 80% of your data and you're assigning for training purpose. And the rest 20%, probably, you'll assign it for testing purpose. So guys, always remember another thing that the training data is always much more than your testing data, obviously because you need to train your machine.

And the more data you feed the machine during the training phase, the better it will be during the testing phase. Obviously, it'll predict better outcomes if it is being trained on more data. Correct? So the model is basically using the machine learning algorithm that predicts the output by using the data fed to it.

Now in the case of predicting rainfall, the output will be a categorical variable, because we'll be predicting whether it's going to rain or not. Okay, so let's say we have an output variable called rain. The two possible values that this variable can take is yes, it's going to rain and no it won't rain. Correct, so that is out come. Our outcome is a classification or a categorical variable. So, for such cases where your outcome is a categorical variable, you'll be using classification algorithms.

Again, example of a classification algorithm is logistic regression or you can also support vector machines, you can use K nearest neighbour, and you can also use naive Bayes, and so on. Now don't worry about these terms, I'll be discussing all these algorithms with you.

But just remember that while you're building a machine learning model, you'll make use of the training data. You'll train the model by using the training data and the machine learning algorithm.

Now like I said, choosing the machine learning algorithm, depends on the problem statement that you're trying to solve because of N number of machine learning algorithms. We'll have to choose the algorithm that is the most suitable for your problem statement.

So, step number six is model evaluation and optimization. Now after you've done building a model by using the training data set, it is finally time to put the model road test. The testing data set is used to check the efficiency of the model and how accurately it can predict the outcome.

So once the accuracy is calculated, any further improvements in the model can be implemented during this stage. The various methods that can help you improve the performance of the model, like you can use parameter tuning and cross validation methods in order to improve the performance of the model.

Now the main things you need to remember during model evaluation and optimization is that model evaluation is nothing but you're testing how well your model can predict the outcome. So, at this stage, you will be using the testing data set. In the previous stage, which is building a model, you'll be using the training data set.

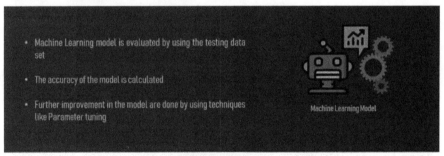

Step 6: Model Evaluation & Optimization
The efficiency of the model is evaluated and any further improvement in the model are implemented.

But in the model evaluation stage, you'll be using the testing data set. Now once you've tested your model, you need to calculate the accuracy. You need to calculate how accurately your model is predicting the outcome.

After that, if you find that you need to improve your model in some way or the other, because the accuracy is not very good, then you'll use methods such as parameter tuning.

Don't worry about these terms, I'll discuss all of this with you, but I'm just trying to make sure that you're understanding the concept behind each of the phases and machine learning.

It's very important you understand each step. Okay, now let's move on and look at the last stage of machine learning, which is predictions. Now, once a model is evaluated and once you've improved it, it is finally used to make predictions.

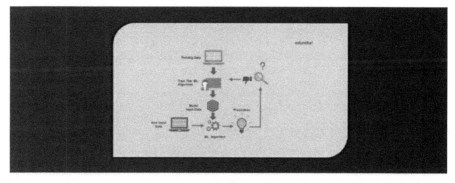

Step 7: Predictions
The final outcome is predicted after performing parameter tuning and improving the accuracy of the model.

The final output can either be a categorical variable or a continuous variable. Now all of this depends on your problem statement. Don't get confused about continuous variables, categorical variables. I'll be discussing all of this. Now in our case, because we're predicting the occurrence of rainfall, the output will be categorical variable.

It's obvious because we're predicting whether it's going to rain or not. The result, we understand that this is a classification problem because we have a categorical variable. So that was the entire machine learning process. Now it's time to learn about the different ways in which machines can learn.

So, let's move ahead and look at the types of machine learning. Now this is one of the most interesting concepts in machine learning, the three different ways in which machines learn. There is something known as supervised learning, unsupervised learning, and reinforcement learning. So we'll go through this one by one.

TYPES OF MACHINE LEARNING

There are three types they are

Supervised Learning

Unsupervised Learning

Reinforcement Learning

SUPERVISED LEARNING

We'll understand what supervised learning is first, and then we'll look at the other two types. So defined supervised learning, it is basically a technique in which we teach or train the machine by using the data, which is well labelled.

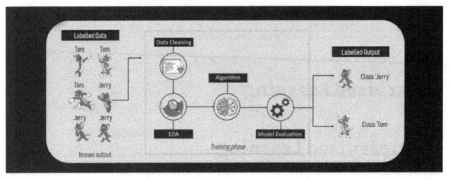

Supervised Learning

Supervised learning is a technique in which we teach or train the machine using data which is well labelled.

Now, in order to understand supervised learning, let's consider a small example. So, as kids, we all needed guidance to solve math problems. A lot of us had trouble solving math problems. So our teachers always help us understand what addition is and how it is done.

Similarly, you can think of supervised learning as a type of machine learning that involves a guide. The label data set is a teacher that will train you to understand the patterns in the data. So, the label data set is nothing but the training data set.

I'll explain more about this in a while. So, to understand supervised learning better, let's look at the figure on the screen. Right here we're feeding the machine image of Tom and Jerry, and the goal is for the machine to identify and classify the images into two classes.

One will contain images of Tom and the other will contain images of Jerry. Now the main thing that you need to note in supervised learning is a training data set. The training data set is going to be very well labelled. Now what do I mean when I say that training data set is labelled.

Basically, what we're doing is we're telling the machine this how Tom looks and this is how Jerry looks. By doing this, you're training the machine by using label data. So the main thing that you're doing is you're labelling every input data that you're feeding to the model.

Basically, you're entire training data set is labelled. Whenever you're giving an image of Tom, there's gonna be a label there saying this is Tom. And when you're giving an image of Jerry, you're saying that this is how Jerry looks.

So, basically, you're guiding the machine and you're telling that, "Listen, this is how Tom looks, "this is how Jerry looks, "and now you need to classify them "into two different classes." That's how supervised learning works. Apart from that, it's the same old process. After getting the input data, you're gonna perform data cleaning.

Then there's exploratory data analysis, followed by creating the model by using the machine learning algorithm, and then this is followed by model evaluation, and finally, your predictions. Now, one more thing to note here is that the output that you get by using supervised learning is also labelled output.

So, basically, you'll get two different classes of name Tom and one of name Jerry, and you'll get them labelled. That is how supervised learning works. The most important thing in supervised learning is that you're training the model by using labelled data set.

Now let's move on and look at unsupervised learning. We look at the same example and understand how unsupervised learning works. So what exactly is unsupervised learning?

UNSUPERVISED LEARNING

Now this involves training by using unlabelled data and allowing the model to act on that information without any guidance. Alright.

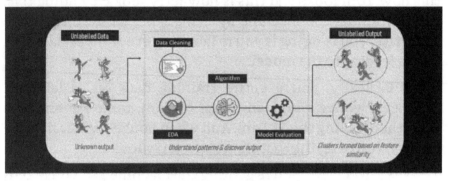

Unsupervised Learning

Unsupervised learning is the training of machine using information that is unlabeled and allowing the algorithm to act on that information without guidance.

Like the name suggest itself, there is no supervision here. It's unsupervised learning. So think of unsupervised learning as a smart kid that learns without any guidance. Okay, in this type of machine learning, the model is not fed with any label data, as in the model has no clue that this is the image of Tom and this is Jerry.

It figures out patterns and the difference between Tom and Jerry on its own by taking in tons and tons of data. Now how do you think the machine identifies this as Tom, and then finally gives us the output like yes this is Tom, this is Jerry. For example, it identifies prominent features of Tom, such as pointy ears, bigger in size, and so on, to understand that this image is of type one.

Similarly, it finds out features in Jerry, and knows that this image is of type two, meaning that the first image is different from the second image. So, what the unsupervised learning algorithm or the model does is it'll form two different clusters. It'll form one cluster which are very similar, and the other cluster which is very different from the first cluster.

That's how unsupervised learning works. So, the important things that you need to know in unsupervised learning is that you're gonna feed the machine unlabelled data. The machine has to understand the patterns and discover the output on its own. And finally, the machine will form clusters based on feature similarity.

REINFORCEMENT LEARNING

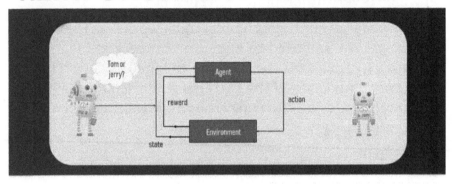

Reinforcement Learning

Reinforcement Learning is a part of Machine learning where an agent is put in an environment and he learns to behave in this environment by performing certain actions and observing the rewards which it gets from those actions.

Reinforcement learning is quite different when compared to supervised and unsupervised learning. What exactly is reinforcement learning? It is a part of machine learning where an agent is put in an environment, and he learns to behave in this environment by performing certain actions, and observing the rewards which is gets from those actions.

To understand what reinforcement learning is, imagine that you were dropped off at an isolate island. What would you do? Now panic. Yes, of course, initially, we'll all panic. But as time passes by, you will learn how to live on the island.

You will explode the environment, you will understand the climate conditions, the type of food that grows there, the dangers of the island so on. This is exactly how reinforcement learning works.

It basically involves an agent, which is you stuck on the island, that is put in an unknown environment, which is the island, where he must learn by observing and performing actions that result in rewards. So reinforcement learning is mainly used in advanced machine learning areas such as self-driving cars and AlphaGo.

I'm sure a lot of you have heard of AlphaGo. So, the logic behind AlphaGo is nothing but reinforcement learning and deep learning. And in reinforcement learning, there is not really any input data given to the agent. All he has to do is he has to explore everything from scratch it's like a new born baby with no information about anything.

He has to go around exploring the environment, and getting rewards, and performing some actions which results in either rewards or in some sort of punishment. Okay. So that sums up the types of machine learning.

Before we move ahead, I'd like to discuss the difference between the three types of machine learning, just to make the concept clear to you all. So let's start by looking at the definitions of each.

SUPERVISED VS UNSUPERVISED VS REINFORCEMENT LEARNING

	Supervised Learning	Unsupervised Learning	Reinforcement Learning
Definition	The machine learns by using labelled data	The machine is trained on unlabelled data without any guidance	An agent interacts with its environment by producing actions & discovers errors or rewards
Type of problems	Regression & Classification	Association & Clustering	Reward based
Type of data	Labelled data	Unlabelled data	No pre-defined data
Training	External supervision	No supervision	No supervision
Approach	Map labelled input to known output	Understand patterns and discover output	Follow trail and error method
Popular algorithms	Linear regression, Logistic regression, Support Vector Machine, KNN, etc	K-means, C-means, etc	Q-Learning, SARSA, etc

Supervised vs Unsupervised vs Reinforcement Learning

In supervised learning, the machine will learn by using the label data. In unsupervised learning, they'll be unlabelled data, and the machine has to learn without any supervision. In reinforcement learning, there'll be an agent which interacts with the environment by producing actions and discover errors or rewards based on his actions.

Now what are the type of problems that can be solved by using supervised, unsupervised, and reinforcement learning. When it comes to supervised learning, the two main types of problems that are solved is regression problems and classification problems. When it comes to unsupervised learning, it is association and clustering problems.

When it comes to reinforcement learning, it's reward-based problems. I'll be discussing regression, classification, clustering, and all of this in the upcoming slides, so don't worry if you don't understand this. Now the type of data which is used in supervised learning is labelled data. In unsupervised learning, it unlabelled. And in reinforcement learning, we have no predefined data set. The agent has to do everything from scratch.

Now the type of training involved in each of these learnings. In supervised learning, there is external supervision, as in there is the labelled data set which acts as a guide for the machine to learn. In unsupervised learning, there's no supervision. Again, in reinforcement learning, there's no supervision at all. Now what is the approach to solve problems by using supervised, unsupervised, and reinforcement learning? In supervised learning, it is simple.

You have to mal the labelled input to the known output. The machine knows what the output looks like. So, you're just labelling the input to the output. In unsupervised learning, you're going to understand the patterns and discover the output.

Here you have no clue about what the input is. It's not labelled. You just have to understand the patterns and you'll have to form clusters and discover the output. In reinforcement learning, there is no clue at all. You'll have to follow the trial and error method.

You'll have to go around your environment. You'll have to explore the environment, and you'll have to try some actions. And only once you perform those actions, you'll know that whether this is a reward-based action or whether this is a punishment-based action.

So, reinforcement learning is totally based on the concept of trial and error. Okay. A popular algorithm on the supervised learning include linear regression, logistic regressions, support vector machines K nearest neighbour, naive Bayes, and so on. Under unsupervised learning, we have the famous K-means clustering method, C-means and all of that.

Under reinforcement learning, we have the famous learning Q-learning algorithm. I'll be discussing these algorithms in the upcoming slides. So let's move on and look at the next topic, which is the types of problems solved using machine learning.

TYPES OF PROBLEMS SOLVED USING MACHINE LEARNING

Now this is what we were talking about earlier when I said regression, classification, and clustering problems. Okay, so let's discuss what exactly I mean by that. In machine learning, all the problems can be classified into three types.

Every problem that is approached in machine learning can be put interest one of these three categories. Okay, so the first type is known as a regression, then we have classification and clustering. So, first, let's look at regression type of problems.

So in this type problem, the output is always a continuous quantity. For example, if you want to predict the speed of a car, given the distance, it is a regression problem. Now a lot of you might not be very aware of what exactly a continuous quantity is.

A continuous quantity is any quantity that can have an infinite range of values. For example, The weight of a person, it is a continuous quantity, because our weight can be 50, 50.1, 50.001, 5.0021, 50.0321 and so on. It can have an infinite range of values, correct? So the type of problem that you have to predict a continuous quantity to make use of regression algorithms. So, regression problems can be solved by using supervised learning algorithms like linear regression.

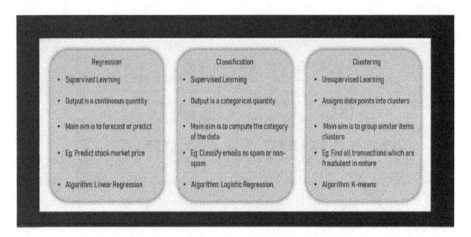

Regression vs Classification vs Clustering

Next, we have classification. Now in this type of problem, the output is always a categorical value. Now when I say categorical value, it can be value such as the gender of a person is a categorical value. Now classifying emails into two classes like spam and non-spam is a classification problem that can be solved by using supervised learning classification algorithms, like support vector machines, naive Bayes, logistic regression, K nearest neighbour, and so on.

So, again, the main aim in classification is to compute the category of the data. Coming to clustering problems. This type of problem involves assigned input into two or more clusters based on feature similarity.

Thus when I read this sentence, you should understand that this is unsupervised learning, because you don't have enough data about your input, and the only option that you have is to form clusters Categories are formed only when you know that your data is of two type. Your input data is labelled and it's of two types, so it's gonna be a classification problem.

But when a clustering problem happens, when you don't have much information about your input, all you have to do is you have to find patterns and you have to understand that data points which are similar are clustered into one group, and data points which are different from the first group are clustered into another group.

That's what clustering is. An example is in Netflix what happens is Netflix clusters their users into similar groups based on their interest, based on their age, geography, and so on. This can be done by using unsupervised learning algorithms like K-means. Okay.

So guys, there were the three categories of problems that can be solved by using machine learning. So, basically, what I'm trying to say is all the problems will fall into one of these categories. So any problem that you give to a machine learning model, it'll fall into one of these categories.

Now to make things a little more interesting, I have collected real world data sets from online resources. And what we're gonna do is we're going to try and understand if this is a regression problem, or a clustering problem, or a classification problem. Okay. Now the problem statement in here is to study the house sales data set, and build a machine learning model that predicts the house pricing index.

Now the most important thing you need to understand when you read a problem statement is you need to understand what is your target variable, what are the possible predictor variable that you'll need. The first thing you should look at is your target variable.

If you want to understand if this a classification, regression, or clustering problem, look at your target variable or your output variable that you're supposed to predict. Here you're supposed to predict the house pricing index. Our house pricing index is obviously a continuous quantity. So as soon as you understand that, you'll know that this is a regression problem.

So, for this, you can make use of the linear regression algorithm, and you can predict the house pricing index. Linear regression is the regression algorithm. It is a supervised learning algorithm. We'll discuss more about it in the further slides.

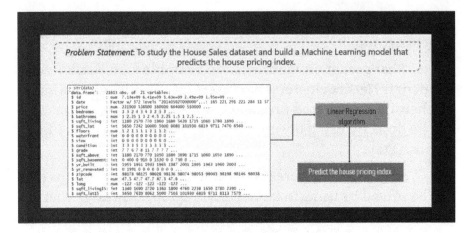

Regression

Let's look at our next problem statement. Here you have to study a bank credit data set, and make a decision about whether to approve the loan of an applicant based on his profile. Now what is your output variable over here? Your output variable is to predict whether you can approve the loan of a applicant or not.

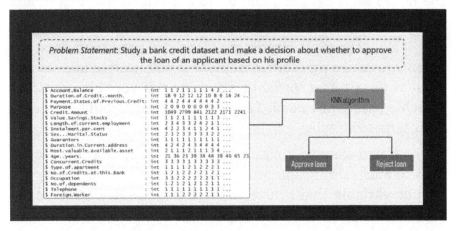

Classification

So, obviously, your output is going to be categorical. It's either going to be yes or no. Yes, is basically approved loan. No is reject loan. So here, you understand that this is a classification problem. Okay. So, you can make use of algorithms like KNN algorithm or you can make use of support vector machines in order to do this.

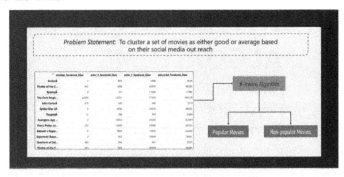

So, support vector machine and KNN which is K nearest neighbour algorithms are basically supervised learning algorithm. We'll talk more about that in the upcoming slides. Moving on to our next problem statement.

Here the problem statement is to cluster a set of movies as either good or average based on the social media outreach. Now if you look properly, your clue is in the question itself. The first line it says is to cluster a set of movies as either good or average.

Now guys, whenever you have a problem statement that is asking you to group the data set into different groups or to form different, different clusters, it's obviously a clustering problem. Right here you can make use of the K-means clustering algorithm, and you can form two clusters. One will contain the popular movies and the other will contain the non-popular movies.

These alright small examples of how you can use machine learning to solve clustering problem, the regression, and classification problems. The key is you need to identify the type of problem first.

SUPERVISED LEARNING ALGORITHMS

Now let's move on and discuss the different types of machine learning algorithms. So we're gonna start by discussing the different supervised learning algorithms.

So, to give you a quick overview, we'll be discussing the linear regression, logistic regression, and decision tree, random forest, naive Bayes classifier, support vector machines, and K nearest neighbour. We'll be discussing these seven algorithms. So without any further delay, let's look at linear regression first.

LINEAR REGRESSION

Now what exactly is a linear regression algorithm? So guys, linear regression is basically a supervised learning algorithm that is used to predict a continuous dependent variable y based on the values of independent variable x. Okay.

The important thing to note here is that the dependent variable y, the variable that you're trying to predict, is always going to be a continuous variable. But the independent variable x, which is basically the predictor variables, these are the variables that you'll be using to predict your output variable, which is nothing but your dependent variable.

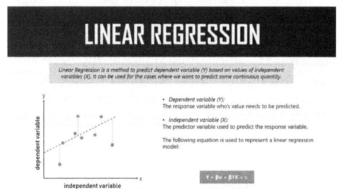

So, your independent variables or your predictive variables can either be continuous or discreet. Okay, there is not such a restriction over here. Okay, they can be either continuous variables or they can be discreet variables. Now, again, I'll tell you what a continuous variable is, in case you've forgotten. It is a vary that has infinite number of possibilities.

So, I'll give you an example of a person's weight. It can be 160 pounds, or they can weigh 160.11 pounds, or 160.1134 pounds and so on. So, the number of possibilities for weight is limitless, and this is exactly what a continuous variable is. Now in order to understand linear regression, let's assume that you want to predict the price of a stock over a period of time.

Okay. For such a problem, you can make use of linear regression by starting the relationship between the dependent variable, which is the stock price, and the independent variable, which is the time. You're trying to predict the stock price over a period of time. So basically, you're gonna check how the price of a stock varies over a period of time.

So, your stock price is going to be your dependent variable or your output variable, and the time is going to be your predictor variable or your independent variable. Let's not confuse it anymore. Your dependent variable is your output variable.

Okay, your independent variable is your input variable or your predictor variable. So in our case, the stock price is obviously a continuous quantity, because the stock price can have an infinite number of values. Now the first step in linear regression is always to draw out a relationship between your dependent and your independent variable by using the best fitting linear length.

We make an assumption that your dependent and independent variable is linearly related to each other. We call it linear regression because both the variables vary linearly, which means that by plotting the relationship between these two variables, we'll get more of a straight line, instead of a curve.

LINEAR REGRESSION

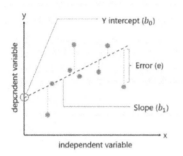

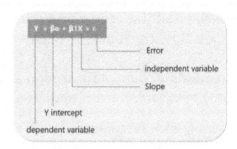

Let's discuss the math behind linear regression. So, this equation over here, it denotes the relationship between your independent variable x, which is here, and your dependent variable y. This is the variable you're trying to predict.

Hopefully, we all know that the equation for a linear line in math is y equals mx plus c. I hope all of you remember math. So, the equation for a linear line in math is y equals to mx plus c. Similarly, the linear regression equation is represented along the same line. Okay, y equals to mx plus c.

There's just a little bit of changes, which I'll tell you what they are. Let's understand this equation properly. So, y basically stands for your dependent variable that you're going to predict. B naught is the y intercept.

Now y intercept is nothing but this point here. Now in this graph, you're basically showing the relationship between your dependent variable y and your independent variable x. Now this is the linear relationship between these two variables.

Okay, now your y intercept is basically the point on the line which starts at the y-axis. This is y interceptor, which is represented by B naught. Now B one or beta is the slope of this line now the slope can either be negative or positive, depending on the relationship between the dependent and independent variable.

The next variable that we have is x. X here represents the independent variable that is used to predict our resulting output variable. Basically, x is used to predict the value of y. Okay. E here denotes the error in the computation. For example, this is the actual line, and these dots here represent the predicted values. Now the distance between these two is denoted by the error in the computation. So, this is the entire equation. It's quite simple, right? Linear regression will basically draw a relationship between your input and your input variable.

That's how simple linear regression was. Now to better understand linear regression, I'll be running a demo in Python. So, guys, before I get started with our practical demo, I'm assuming that most of you have a good understanding of Python, because explaining Python is going to be out of the scope of today's session. But if some of you are not familiar with the Python language, I'll leave a couple of links in the end of the book.

LINEAR REGRESSION DEMO

Those will be related to Python programming. You can go through those links, understand Python, and then maybe try to understand the demo. But I'd be explaining the logic part of the demo in depth. So, the main thing that we're going to do here is try and understand linear regression.

So, it's okay if you do not understand Python for now. I'll try to explain as much as I can. But if you still want to understand this in a better way, I'll leave a couple of links in the end of the book you can go to those videos. Let me just share some screenshot of my computer with you. I hope all of you can see the image helpful.

Now in this linear regression demo, what we're going to do is we're going to form a linear relationship between the maximum temperature and minimum temperature on a particular date. We're just going to do weather forecasting here. So our task is to predict the maximum temperature, taking input feature as minimum temperature.

So, I'm just going to try and make you understand linear regression through this demo. Okay, we'll see how it actually works practically. Before I get started with the demo, let me tell you something about the data set.

Our data set is stored in this path basically. The name of the data set is weather.csv. Okay, now, this contains data on whether conditions recorded on each day at various weather stations around the world. Okay, the information include precipitation, snowfall, temperatures, wind speeds, and whether the day included any thunderstorm or other poor weather conditions.

So, our first step in any demo for that matter will be to import all the libraries that are needed. So, we're gonna begin our demo by importing all the required libraries. After that, we're going to read in our data. Our data will be stored in this variable called data set, and we're going to use a read.csv function since our data set is in the CSV format. After that, I'll be showing you how the data set looks.

We'll also look at the data set in depth. Now let me just show you the output first. Let's run this demo and see first. We're getting a couple of plots which I'll talk about in a while. So, we can ignore this warning. It has nothing to do with... So, first of all, we're printing the shape of our data set. So, when we print the shape of our data set, this is the output that we get.

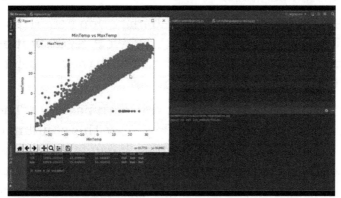

So, basically, this shows that we have around 12,000 rows and 31 columns in our data set. The 31 columns basically represent the predictor variables. So, you can say that we have

31 predictor variables in order to protect the weather conditions on a particular date.

So, guys, the main aim in this problem segment is weather forecast. We're going to predict the weather by using a set of predictor variables. So, these are the different types of predictor variables that we have. Okay, we have something known as maximum temperature.

So, this is what our data set looks like. Now what I'm doing in this block of code is... What we're doing is we're plotting our data points on a 2D graph in order to understand our data set and see if we can manually find any relationship between the variables. Here we've taken minimum temperature and maximum temperature for doing our analysis.

So, let's just look at this plot. Before that, let me just comment all of these other plots, so that you see on either graph that I'm talking about. So, when you look at this graph, this is basically the graph between your minimum temperature and your maximum temperature. Maximum temperature is dependent variable that you're going to predict. This is y. And your minim temperature is your x. It's basically your independent variable.

If you look at this graph, you can see that there is a sort of linear relationship between the two, except there are a little bit of outliers here and there. There are a few data points which are a little bit random. But apart from that, there is a pretty linear relationship between your minimum temperature and your maximum temperature.

So, by this graphic, you can understand that you can easily solve this problem using linear regression, because our data is very linear. I can see a clear straight line over here. This is our first graph. Next, what I'm doing is I'm just checking the average and maximum temperature that we have.

I'm just looking at the average of our output variable. Okay. So guys, what we're doing here right now is just exploratory data analysis. We're trying to understand our data. We're trying to see the relationship between our input variable and our output variable.

We're trying to see the mean or the average of the output variable. All of this is necessary to understand our data set. So, this is what our average maximum temperature looks like. So if we try to understand where exactly this is, so our average maximum temperature is somewhere between 28 and I would say between 30. 28 and 32, somewhere there.

So, you can say that average maximum temperature lies between 25 and 35. And so that is our average maximum temperature. Now that you know a little bit about the data set, you know that there is a very good linear relationship between your input variable and your output variable.

Now what you're going to do is you're going to perform something known as data splicing. Let me just comment that for you. This section is nothing but data splicing. So for those of you who are paying attention, know that data splicing is nothing but splitting your data set into training and testing data.

Now before we do that, I mentioned earlier that we'll be only using two variables, because we're trying to understand the relationship between the minimum temperature and maximum temperature. I'm doing this because I want you to understand linear regression in the simplest way possible.

So guys, in order to make understand linear regression, I have just derived only two variables from a data set. Even though when we check the structure of a data set, we had around 31 features, meaning that we had 31 variables which include my predictor variable and my target variable.

we had 30 predictor variables and we had one target variable, which is your maximum temperature. So, what I'm doing here is I'm only considering these two variables, because I want to show you exactly how linear regression works. So, here what I'm doing is I'm basically extracting only these two variables from our data set, storing it in x and y.

After that, I'm performing data splicing. So here, I'm basically splitting the data into training and testing data, and remember one point that I am assigning 20% of the data to our testing data set, and the remaining 80% is assigned for training. That's how training works. We assign maximum data set for training.

We do this because we want the machine learning model or the machine learning algorithm to train better on data. We wanted to take as much data as possible, so that it can predict the outcome properly. So, to repeat it again for you, so here we're just splitting the data into training and testing data set.

one more thing to note here is that we're splitting 80% of the data from training, and we're assigning the 20% of the data to test data. The test size variable, this variable that you see, is what is used to specify the proportion of the test set.

Now after splitting the data into training and testing set, finally, the time is to train our algorithm. For that, we need to import the linear regression class. We need to instantiate it and call the fit method along with the training data. This is our linear regression class, and we're just creating an instance of the linear regression class.

So, guys, a good thing about Python is that you have pre-defined classes for your algorithms, and you don't have call your algorithms. Instead, all you have to do, is you call this class linear regression class, and you have to create an instance of it.

Here I'm basically creating something known as a regressor. And all you have to do is you have to call the fit method along with your training data. So, this is my training data, x train and y train contain my training data, and I'm calling our linear regression instance, which is regressor, along with this data set.

So here, basically, we're building the model. We're doing nothing but building the model. Now, one of the major things that linear regression model does is it finds the best value for the intercept and the slope, which results in a line that best fits the data. I've discussed what intercept and slope is. So, if you want to see the intercept and the slope calculated by our linear regression model, we just have to run this line of code.

And let's looks at the output for that. So, our intercept is around 10.66 and our coefficient, these are also known as beta coefficients, coefficient is nothing but what we discussed, beta naught. These are beta values. Now this will just help you understand the significance of your input variables. Now what this coefficient value means is, see, the coefficient value is around 0.92.

This means that for every one unit changed of your minimum temperature, the change in the maximum temperature is around 0.92. This will just show you how significant your input variable is. So, for every one-unit change in your minimum temperature, the change in the maximum temperature will be around 0.92. I hope you've understood this part.

Now that we've trained our algorithm, it's trying to make some predictions. To do so, what we'll use is we'll use our test data set, and we'll see how accurately our algorithm predicts the percentage score. Now to make predictions, we have this line of code.

Predict is basically a predefined function in Python. And all you're going to do is you're going to pass your testing data set to this. Now what you'll do is you'll compare the actual output values, which is basically stored in your y test.

And you'll compare these to the predicted values, which is in y prediction. And you'll store these comparisons in our data frame called df. And all I'm doing here is I'm printing the data frame. So, if you look at the output, this is what it looks like.

These are your actual values and these are the values that you predicted by building that model. So, if your actual value is 28, you predicted around 33, here your actual value is 31, meaning that your maximum temperature is 31. And you predicted a maximum temperature of 30. Now, these values are actually pretty close. I feel like the accuracy is pretty good over here.

Now in some cases, you see a lot of variance, like 23. Here it's 15. Right here it's 22. Here it's 11. But such cases are very often. And the best way to improve your accuracy I would say is by training a model with more data. Alright. You can also view this comparison in the form of a plot. Let's see how that looks.

So, basically, this is a bar graph that shows our actual values and our predicted values. Blue is represented by your actual values, and orange is represented by your predicted values. At places you can see that we've predicted pretty well, like the predictions are pretty close to the actual values.

In some cases, the predictions are varying a little bit. So in a few places, it is actually varying, but all of this depends on your input data as well. When we saw the input data, also we saw a lot of variation. We saw a couple of outliers.

So, all that also might affect your output. But then this is how you build machine learning models. Initially, you're never going to get a really good accuracy. What you should do is you have to improve your training process.

That's the best way you can predict better, either you use a lot of data, train your model with a lot of data, or you use other methods like parameter tuning, or basically you try and find another predictor variable that'll help you more in predicting your output.

To me, this looks pretty good. Now let me show you another plot. What we're doing is we're drawing a straight-line plot. Okay, let's see how it looks. So, guys, this straight line represents a linear relationship. Now let's say you get a new data point.

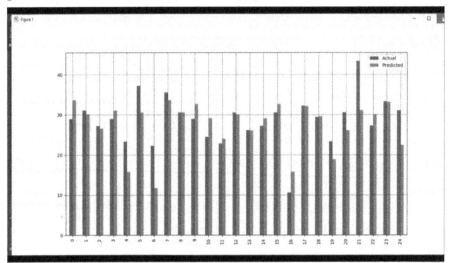

Okay, let's say the value of x is around 20. So, by using this line, you can predict that four a minimum temperature of 20, your maximum temperature would be around 25 or something like that. So, we basically drew a linear relationship between our input and output variable over here. And the final step is to evaluate the performance of the algorithm.

This step is particularly important to compare how well different algorithms perform on a particular data set. Now for regression algorithms, three evaluation metrics are used. We have something known as mean absolute error, mean squared error, and root mean square error.

LINEAR REGRESSION

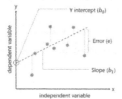
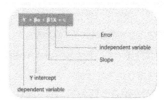

Now mean absolute error is nothing but the absolute value of the errors. Your mean squared error is a mean of the squared errors. That's all. It's basically you read this and you understand what the error means.

A root mean squared error is the square root of the mean of the squared errors. Okay. So these are pretty simple to understand your mean absolute error, your mean squared errors, your root mean squared error.

Now, luckily, we don't have to perform these calculations manually. We don't have to code each of these calculations. The cycle on library comes with prebuilt functions that can be used to find out these values.

when you run this code, you will get these values for each of the errors. You'll get around 3.19 as the mean absolute error. Your mean squared error is around 17.63. Your root mean squared error is around 4.19. Now these error values basically show that our model accuracy is not very precise, but it's still able to make a lot of predictions.

We can draw a good linear relationship. Now in order to improve the efficiency at all, there are a lot of methods like this, parameter tuning and all of that, or basically you can train your model with a lot more data. Apart from that, you can use other predictor variables, or maybe you can study the relationship between other predictor variables and your maximum temperature variable.

LOGISTIC REGRESSION

There are a lot of ways to improve the efficiency of the model. But for now, I just wanted to make you understand how linear regression works, and I hope all of you have a good idea about this. I hope all of you have a good understanding of how linear regression works. This is a small demo about it. If any of you still have any doubts, regarding linear regression, please watch a video that link will be given in the end of the book.

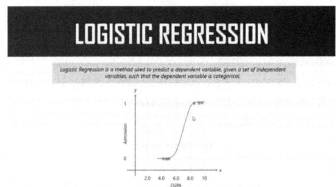

We'll try and solve all your errors. So, if you look at this equation, we calculated everything here. we drew a relationship between y and x, which is basically x was our minimum temperature, y was our maximum temperature. We also calculated the slope and the intercept. And we also calculated the error in the end. We calculated mean squared error we calculated the root mean squared error.

We also calculate the mean absolute error. So that was everything about linear regression. This was a simple linear regression model. Now let's move on and look at our next algorithm, which is a logistic regression. Now, in order to understand why we use logistic regression, let's consider a small scenario. Let's say that your little sister is trying to get into grad school and you want to predict whether she'll get admitted in her dream school or not.

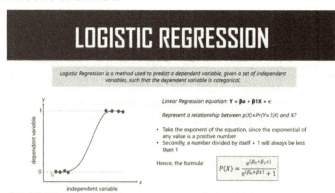

Okay, so based on her CGPA and the past data, you can use logistic regression to foresee the outcome. So logistic regression will allow you to analyse the set of variables and predict a categorical outcome. Since here we need to predict whether she will get into a school or not, which is a classification problem, logistic regression will be used.

Now I know the first question in your head is, why are we not using linear regression in this case? The reason is that linear regression is used to predict a continuous quantity, rather than a categorical one. Here we're going to predict whether or not your sister is going to get into grad school. So that is clearly a categorical outcome.

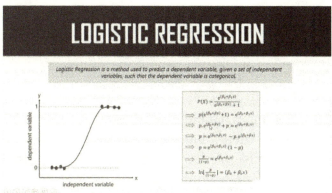

So, when the result in outcome can take only classes of values, like two classes of values, it is sensible to have a model that predicts the value as either zero or one, or in a probability form that ranges between zero and one.

linear regression does not have this ability. If you use linear regression to model a binary outcome, the resulting model will not predict y values in the range of zero and one, because linear regression works on continuous dependent variables, and not on categorical variables. That's why we make use of logistic regression.

So, understand that linear regression was used to predict continuous quantities, and logistic regression is used to predict categorical quantities. Okay, now one major confusion that everybody has is people keep asking me why is logistic regression called logistic regression when it is used for classification. The reason it is named logistic regression is because its primary technique is very similar to logistic regression.

There's no other reason behind the naming. It belongs to the general linear models. It belongs to the same class as linear regression, but that is not the other reason behind the name logistic regression. Logistic regression is mainly used for classification purpose, because here you'll have to predict a dependent variable which is categorical in nature.

So, this is mainly used for classification. So, to define logistic regression for you, logistic regression is a method used to predict a dependent variable y, given an independent variable x, such that the dependent variable is categorical, meaning that your output is a categorical variable. So, obviously, this is classification algorithm.

So, guys, again, to clear your confusion, when I say categorical variable, I mean that it can hold values like one or zero, yes or no, true or false, and so on. So, basically, in logistic regression, the outcome is always categorical.

Now, how does logistic regression work? So guys, before I tell you how logistic regression works, take a look at this graph. Now I told you that the outcome in a logistic regression is categorical. Your outcome will either be zero or one, or it'll be a probability that ranges between zero and one. So, that's why we have this S curve.

Now some of you might think that why do we have an S curve. We can obviously have a straight line. We have something known as a sigmoid curve, because we can have values ranging between zero and one, which will basically show the probability. So, maybe your output will be 0.7, which is a probability value. If it is 0.7, it means that your outcome is basically one.

So that's why we have this sigmoid curve like this. Okay. Now I'll explain more about this in depth in a while. Now, in order to understand how logistic regression works, first, let's take a look at the linear regression equation. This was the logistic regression equation that we discussed. Y here stands for the dependent variable that needs to be predicted beta naught is nothing by the y intercept. Beta one is nothing but the slope.

And X here represents the independent variable that is used to predict y. That E denotes the error on the computation. So, given the fact that x is the independent variable and y is the dependent variable, how can we represent a relationship between x an y so that y ranges only between zero and one? Here this value basically denotes probably of y equal to one, given some value of x.

So here, because this PR, denotes probability and this value basically denotes that the probability of y equal to one, given some value of x, this is what we need to find out.

Now, if you wanted to calculate the probability using the linear regression model, then the probably will look something like P of X equal to beta naught plus beta one into X. P of X will be equal to beta naught plus beta one into X, where P of X nothing but your probability of getting y equal to one, given some value of x.

So, the logistic regression equation is derived from the

same equation, except we need to make a few alterations, because the output is only categorical. So, logistic regression does not necessarily calculate the outcome as zero or one. I mentioned this before. Instead, it calculates the probability of a variable falling in the class zero or class one.

So that's how we can conclude that the resulting variable must be positive, and it should lie between zero and one, which means that it must be less than one. So to meet these conditions, we have to do two things. First, we can take the exponent of the equation, because taking an exponential of any value will make sure that you get a positive number.

Correct? Secondly, you have to make sure that your output is less than one. So, a number divided by itself plus one will always be less than one. So that's how we get this formula First, we take the exponent of the equation, beta naught plus beta one plus x and then we divide it by that number plus one. So this is how we get this formula.

Now the next step is to calculate something known as a logic function. Now the logic function is nothing, but it is a link function that is represented as an S curve or as a sigmoid curve that ranges between the value zero and one.

It basically calculates the probability of the output variable. So if you look at this equation, it's quite simple. What we have done here is we just cross multiply and take each of our beta naught plus beta one into x as common. The RHS denotes the linear equation for the independent variables. The LHS represents the odd ratio.

So, if you compute this entire thing, you'll get this final value, which is basically your logistic regression equation. Your RHS here denotes the linear equation for independent variables, and your LHS represents the odd ratio which is also known as the logic function.

I told you that logic function is basically a function that represents an S curve that bring zero and one. this will make sure that our value ranges between zero and one. So, in logistic regression, on increasing this X by one measure, it changes the logic by a factor of beta naught. It's the same thing as I showed you in logistic regression.

So, guys, that's how you derive the logistic regression equation. So, if you have any doubts regarding these equations, please watch the links that are given in the end of the book, and I'll get back to you, and I'll clear that out. So, to sum it up, logistic regression is used for classification.

The output variable will always be a categorical variable. We also saw how you derive the logistic regression equation. And one more important thing is that the relationship between the variables and a logistic regression is denoted as an S curve which is also knows as a sigmoid curve, and also the outcome does not necessarily have to be calculated as zero or one.

It can be calculating as a probability that the output lies in class one or class zero. So, your output can be a probability ranging between zero and one. That's why we have a sigmoid curve. So, I hope all of you are clear with logistic regression.

Now I won't be showing you the demo right away. I'll explain a couple of more classification algorithms. Then I'll show you a practical demo where we'll use multiple classification algorithms to solve the same problem. Again, we'll also calculate the accuracy and se which classification algorithm is doing the best. Now the next algorithm I'm gonna talk about is decision tree.

DECISION TREE

DECISION TREE

A Decision Tree is a Supervised Machine Learning algorithm which looks like an inverted tree, wherein each node represents a **predictor variable** (feature), the link between the nodes represents a **Decision** and each leaf node represents an **outcome** (response variable).

Decision tree is one of my favourite algorithms, because it's very simple to understand how a decision tree works. So guys, before this, we discussed linear regression, which was a regression algorithm. Then we discussed logistic regression, which is a classification algorithm.

Remember, don't get confused just because it has the name logistic regression. Okay, it is a classification algorithm. Now we're discussing decision tree, which is again a classification algorithm. Okay. So what exactly is a decision tree? Now a decision tree is, again, a supervised machine learning algorithm which looks like an inverted tree wherein each node represents a predictor variable, and the link between the node represents a decision, and each leaf node represents an outcome.

DECISION TREE

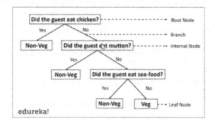

edureka!

Root Node: The root node is the starting point of a tree. At this point, the first split is performed.

Internal Nodes: Each internal node represents a decision point (predictor variable) that eventually leads to the prediction of the outcome.

Leaf/ Terminal Nodes: Leaf nodes represent the final class of the outcome and therefore they're also called terminating nodes.

Branches: Branches are connections between nodes, they're represented as arrows. Each branch represents a response such as yes or no.

Now I know that's a little confusing, so let me make you understand what a decision tree is with the help of an example. Let's say that you hosted a huge party, and you want to know how many of your gusts are non-vegetarians.

So, to solve this problem, you can create a simple decision tree. Now if you look at this figure over here, I've created a decision tree that classifies a guest as either vegetarian or nonvegetarian. Our last outcome here is non-veg or veg.

Here you understand that this is a classification algorithm, because here you're predicting a categorical value. Each node over here represents a predictor variable. So, eat chicken is one variable, eat mutton is one variable, seafood is another variable. So, each node represents a predictor variable that will help you conclude whether or not a guest is a non-vegetarian.

Now as you traverse down the tree, you'll make decisions that each node until you reach the dead end. Okay, that's how it works. So, let's say we got a new data point. Now we'll pass it through the decision tree. The first variable is doing the guest eat the chicken? If yes, then he's a non-vegetarian.

If no, then you'll pass it to the next variable, which is did the guest eat mutton? If yes, then he's a non-vegetarian. If no, then you'll pass it to the next variable, which is seafood. If he ate seafood, then he is a non-vegetarian. If no, then he's a vegetarian.

This is how a decision tree works. It's a very simple algorithm that you can easily understand. It has drawn out letters, which is very easy to understand. Now let's understand the structure of a decision tree.

I just showed you an example of how the decision tree works. Now let me take the same example and tell you the structure for decision tree. So, first of all, we have something known as the root node. Okay. The root node is the starting point of a decision tree.

Here you'll perform the first split and split it into two other nodes or three other nodes, depending on your problem statement. So the top most node is known as your root node. Now guys, about the root node, the root node is assigned to a variable that is very significant, meaning that that variable is very important in predicting the output. Okay, so you assign a variable that you think is the most significant at the root node.

After that, we have something known as internal nodes. So each internal node represents a decision point that eventually leads to the output. Internal nodes will have other predictor variables. Each of these are nothing predictor variables.

I just made it into a question otherwise these are just predictor variables. Those are internal nodes. Terminal nodes, also known as the leaf node, represent the final class of the output variable, because these are basically your outcomes, non-veg and vegetarian.

Branches are nothing but connections between nodes. Okay, these connections are links between each node is known as a branch, and they're represented by arrows. So each branch will have some response to it, either yes or no, true or false, one or zero, and so on.

Okay. So, guys, this is the structure of a decision tree. It's pretty understandable. Now let's move on and we'll understand how the decision tree algorithm works. Now there are many ways to build a decision tree, but I'll be focusing on something known as the ID3 algorithm. Okay, this is something known as the ID3 algorithm.

That is one of the ways in which you can build the decision tree. ID3 stands for Iterative Dichotomise 3 algorithm, which is one of the most effective algorithms used to build a decision tree. It uses the concepts of entropy and information gain in order to build a decision tree. Now you don't have to know what exactly the ID3 algorithm is.

It's just a concept behind building a decision tree. Now the ID3 algorithm has around six defined steps in order to build a decision tree. So the first step is you will select the best attribute. Now what do you mean by the best attribute? So, attribute is nothing but the predictor variable over here. So you'll select the best predictor variable.

Let's call it A. After that, you'll assign this A as a decision variable for the root node. Basically, you'll assign this predictor variable A at the root node. Next, what you'll do is for each value of A, you'll build a descendant of the node.

Now these three steps, let's look at it with the previous example. Now here the best attribute is eaten chicken. Okay, this is my best attribute variable over here. So I selected that attribute. And what is the next step? Step two was assigned that as a decision variable. So I assigned eat chick as the decision variable at the root node.

Now you might be wondering how do I know which is the best attribute. I'll explain all of that in a while. So, what we did is we assigned this other root node. After that, step number three says for each value of A, build a descendant of the node.

So, for each value of this variable, build a descendant node. So, this variable can take two values, yes and no. So for each of these values, I build a descendant node. Step number four, assign classification labels to the leaf node. To your leaf node, I have assigned classification one as non-veg, and the other is veg. That is step number four.

Step number five is if data is correctly classified, then you stop at that. However, if it is not, then you keep iterating over the tree, and keep changing the position of the predictor variables in the tree, or you change the root node also in order to get the correct output. So now let me answer this question.

What is the best attribute? What do you mean by the best attribute or the best predictor variable? Now the best attribute is the one that separates the data into different classes, most effectively, or it is basically a feature that best splits the data set. Now the next question in your head must be how do I decide which variable or which feature best splits the data.

To do this, there are two important measures. There's something known as information gain and there's something known as entropy. Now guys, in order to understand information gain and entropy, we look at a simple problem statement. This data represents the speed of a car based on certain parameters.

So, our problem statement here is to study the data set and create a decision tree that classifies the speed of the car as either slow or fast. So, our predictor variables here are road type, obstruction, and speed limit, and or response variable, or our output variable is speed. So, we'll be building a decision tree using these variables in order to predict the speed of car.

Now like I mentioned earlier, we must first begin by deciding a variable that best splits the data set and assign that particular variable to the root node and repeat the same thing for other nodes as well. So, step one, like we discussed earlier, is to select the best attribute A.

Now, how do you know which variable best separates the data? The variable with the highest information gains best derives the data into the desired output classes. First of all, we'll calculate two measures.

We'll calculate the entropy and the information gain. Now this is where it tell you what exactly entropy is, and what exactly information gain is. Now entropy is basically used to measure the impurity or the uncertainty present in the data. It is used to decide how a decision tree can split the data. Information gain, on the other hand, is the most significant measure which is used to build a decision tree.

It indicates how much information a particular variable gives us about the final outcome. So information gain is important, because it is used to choose a variable that best splits the data at each node for a decision tree.

INFORMATION GAIN & ENTROPY

Calculating IG of parent node (Speed of car)

Similarly for p(fast),

p(fast) = no. of 'fast' outcomes in the parent node / total number of outcomes

$$P_{fast} = \frac{2}{4} = 0.5$$

Road type	Obstruction	Speed limit	Speed
steep	yes	yes	slow
steep	no	yes	slow
flat	yes	no	fast
steep	no	no	fast

Therefore, the entropy of the parent node is:

$$Entropy_{parent} = -\Sigma p_{slow}log_2(p_{slow}) + p_{fast}log_2(p_{fast})$$

Entropy(parent) = – {0.5 log2(0.5) + 0.5 log2(0.5)} = – {-0.5 + (-0.5)} = 1

Now the variable with the highest information gain will be used to split the data at the root node. Now in our data set, there are four observations. So what we're gonna do is we'll start by calculating the entropy and information gain for each of the predictor variable.

So, we're gonna start by calculating the information gain and entropy for the road type variable. In our data set, you can see that there are four observations. There are four observations in the road type column, which corresponds to the four

PON MAHESH

labels in the speed column. So we're gonna begin by calculating the information gain of the parent node.

INFORMATION GAIN & ENTROPY

Calculating IG of child node (Road Type)

Entropy of right side child node (fast):

Entropy of left side child node (slow, slow, fast):

P(slow) = 2/3 = 0.667
P(fast) = 1/3 = 0.334

Therefore, the entropy is:

Entropy(left child node) = − {0.667 log2(0.667) + 0.334 log2(0.334)}
= − {-0.38 + (-0.52)} = 0.9

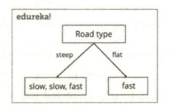

The parent node is nothing but the speed of the care node. This is our output variable, correct? It'll be used to show whether the speed of the car is slow or fast. So to find out the information gain of the speed of the car variable, we'll go through a couple of steps.

Now we know that there are four observations in this parent node. First, we have slow. Then again, we have slow, fast, and fast. Now, out of these four observations, we have two classes. So, two observations belong to the class slow, and two observations belong to the class fast. So that's how you calculate P slow and P fast. P slow is nothing by the fraction of slow outcomes in the parent node, and P fast is the fraction of fast outcomes in the parent node.

INFORMATION GAIN & ENTROPY

Calculating IG of child node (Road Type)

Information Gain = entropy(parent) - [weighted average] * entropy(children)

Therefore,

Information gain(Road type) = 1 - 0.675 = 0.325

So by using the above methodology, you must get the following values for each predictor variable:

- Information gain(Road type) = 1 - 0.675 = 0.325
- Information gain(Obstruction) = 1 - 1 = 0
- **Information gain(Speed limit) = 1 - 0 = 1**

And the formula to calculate P slow is the number of slow outcomes in the parent node divided by the total number of outcomes. So the number of slow outcomes in the parent node is two, and the total number of outcomes is four. We have four observations in total. So that's how we get P of slow as 0.5. Similarly, for P of fast, you'll calculate the number of fast outcomes divided by the total number of outcomes.

So again, two by four, you'll get 0.5. The next thing you'll do is you'll calculate the entropy of this node. So to calculate the entropy, this is the formula. All you have to do is you have to substitute the, you'll have to substitute the value in this formula. So P of slow we're substituting as 0.5. Similarly, P of fast as 0.5. Now when you substitute the value, you'll get a answer of one. So the entropy of your parent node is one.

So after calculating the entropy of the parent node, we'll calculate the information gain of the child node. Now guys, remember that if the information gain of the road type variable is great than the information gain of all the other predictor variables, only then the root node can be split by using the road type variable.

So, to calculate the information gain of road type variable, we first need to split the root node by sing the road type variable. We're just doing this in order to check if the road type variable is giving us maximum information about a data. Okay, so if you notice that road type has two outcomes, it has two values, either steep or flat.

INFORMATION GAIN & ENTROPY

Problem Statement: To study the data set and create a Decision Tree that classifies the speed of a car as either slow or fast,

Road type	Obstruction	Speed limit	Speed
steep	yes	yes	slow
steep	no	yes	slow
flat	yes	no	fast
steep	no	no	fast

Now go back to our data set. So here what you can notice is whenever the road type is steep, so first what we'll do is we'll check the value of speed that we get when the road type is steep. So, first, observation.

You see that whenever the road type is steep, you're getting a speed of slow. Similarly, in the second observation, when the road type is steep, you'll get a value of slow again. If the road type is flat, you'll get an observation of fast.

And again, if it is steep, there is a value of fast. So, for three steep values, we have slow, slow, and fast. And when the road type is flat, we'll get an output of fast. That's exactly what I've done in this decision tree. So, whenever the road type is steep, you'll get slow, slow or fast.

And whenever the road type is flat, you'll get fast. Now the entropy of the right-hand side is zero. Entropy is nothing but the uncertainty. There's no uncertainty over here. Because as soon as you see that the road type is flat, your output is fast. So, there's no uncertainty.

But when the road type is steep, you can have any one of the following outcomes, either your speed will be slow or it can be fast. So, you'll start by calculating the entropy of both RHS and LHS of the decision tree. So, the entropy for the right side child node will be zero, because there's no uncertainty here.

Immediately, if you see that the road type is flat, your speed of the car will be fast. Okay, so there's no uncertainty here, and therefore your entropy becomes zero. Now entropy for the left-hand side is we'll again have to calculate the fraction of P slow and the fraction of P fast.

So out of three observations, in two observations we have slow. That's why we have two by three over here. Similarly, for P fast, we have one P fast divided by the total number of observations which are three. So out of these three, we have two slows and one fast.

When you calculate P slow and P fast, you'll get these two values. And then when you substitute the entropy in this formula, you'll get the entropy as 0.9 for the road type variable. I hope you all are understanding this. I'll go through this again.

So, basically, here we are calculating the information gain and entropy for road type variable. Whenever you consider road type variable, there are two values, steep and flat. And whenever the value for road type is steep, you'll get anyone of these three outcomes, either you'll get slow, slow, or fast. And when the road type is flat, your outcome will be fast.

Now because there is no uncertainty whenever the road type is flat, you'll always get an outcome of fast. This means that the entropy here is zero, or the uncertainty value here is zero. But here, there is a lot of uncertainty. So whenever your road type is steep, your output can either be slow or it can be fast.

So, finally, you get the Python as 0.9. So in order to calculate the information gain of the road type variable. You need to calculate the weighted average. I'll tell you why. In order to calculate the information gain, you need to know the entropy of the parent, which we calculate as one, minus the weighted average into the entropy of the children.

Okay. So for this formula, you need to calculate all of these values. So, first of all, you need to calculate the entropy of the weighted average. Now the total number of outcomes in the parent node we saw were four. The total number of outcomes in the left child node were three.

And the total number of outcomes in the right child node was one. Correct? In order to verify this with you, the total number of outcomes in the parent node are four. One, two, three, and four. Coming to the child node, which is the road type, the total number of outcomes on the right-hand side of the child node is one.

And the total number of outcomes on the left-hand side of the child node is three. That's exactly what I've written over here. Alright, I hope you all understood these three values. After that, all you have to do is you have to substitute these values in this formula.

So when you do that, you'll get the entropy of the children with weighted average will be around 0.675. Now just substitute the value in this formula. So if you calculate the information gain of the road type variable, you'll get a value of 0.325.

Now by using the same method, you're going to calculate the information gain for each of the predictor variable, for road type, for obstruction, and for speed limit. Now when you follow the same method and you calculate the information gain; you'll get these values.

Now what does this information gain for road type equal to 0.325 denote? Now the value 0.325 for road type denotes that we're getting very little information gain from this road type variable. And for obstruction, we literally have information gain of zero. Similarly, information gained for speed limit is one.

This is the highest value we've got for information gain. This means that we'll have to use the speed limit variable at our root node in order to split the data set. So guys, don't get confused whichever variable gives you the maximum information gain. That variable has to be chosen at the root node. So that's why we have the root node as speed limit. So if you've maintained the speed limit, then you're going to go slow.

But if you haven't maintained the speed limit, then the speed of your car is going to be fast. Your entropy is literally zero, and your information is one, meaning that you can use this variable at your root node in order to split the data set, because speed limit gives you the maximum information gain.

So, guys, I hope this use case is clear to all of you. To sum everything up, I'll just repeat the entire thing to you all once more. So basically, here you were given a problem statement in order to create a decision tree that classifies the speed of a car as either slow or fast.

So, you were given three predictor variables and this was your output variable. Information gained in entropy are basically two measures that are used to decide which variable will be assigned to the root node of a decision tree.

Okay. So guys, as soon as you look at the data set, if you compare these two columns, that is speed limit and speed, you'll get an output easily. Meaning that if you're maintaining speed limit, you're going to go slow. But if you aren't maintaining speed limit, you're going to a fast. So here itself we can understand the speed limit has no uncertainty.

So, every time you've maintained your speed limit, you will be going slow, and every time your outside or speed limit, you will be going fast. It's as simple as that. So how did you start? So, you started by calculating the entropy of the parent node.

You calculated the entropy of the parent node, which came down to one. Okay. After that, you calculated the information gain of each of the child nodes. In order to calculate the information gain of the child node, you start by calculating the entropy of the right-hand side and the left-hand side of the decision tree.

Okay. Then you calculate the entropy along with the weighted average. You substitute these values in the information gain formula, and you get the information gain for each of the predictor variables. So after you get the information gain of each of the predictor variables, you check which variable gives you the maximum information gain, and you assign that variable to your root node. It's as simple as that. So, guys, that was all about decision trees. Now let's look at our next classification algorithm

RANDOM FOREST

Now first of all, what is a random forest? Random forest basically builds multiple decision trees and glues them together to get a more accurate and stable prediction. Now if already have decision trees and random forest is nothing but a collection of decision tree, why do we have to use a random forest when we already have decision tree? There are three main reasons why random forest is used.

RANDOM FOREST

Random forest builds multiple decision trees (called the forest) and glues them together to get a more accurate and stable prediction.

Why Random Forest?

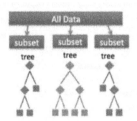

Now even though decision trees are convenient and easily implemented, they are not as accurate as random forest. Decision trees work very effectively with the training data, backup they're not flexible when it comes to classifying a new sample.

RANDOM FOREST

We're going to use this data set to create a Random Forest that predicts if a person has heart disease or not.

Blood Flow	Blocked Arteries	Chest Pain	Weight	Heart Disease
Abnormal	No	No	130	No
Normal	Yes	Yes	195	Yes
Normal	No	Yes	218	No
Abnormal	Yes	Yes	180	Yes

Now this happens because of something known as over-fitting. Now overfitting is a problem that is seen with decision trees. It's something that commonly occurs when we use decision trees. Now overfitting occurs when a model studies a training data to such an extent that it negatively influences the performance of the model on a new data.

Now this means that the disturbance in the training data is recorded, and it is learned as concept by the model. If there's any disturbance or any thought of noise in the training data or any error in the training data, that is also studied by the model.

The problem here is that these concepts do not apply to the testing data, and it negatively impacts the model's ability to classify new data. So to sum it up, overfitting occurs whenever your model learns the training data, along with all the disturbance in the training data.

So it basically memorized the training data. And whenever a new data will be given to your model, it will not predict the outcome very accurately. now this is a problem seen in decision trees. Okay. But in random forest, there's something known as bagging.

Now the basic idea behind bagging is to reduce the variations and the predictions by combining the result of multiple decision trees on different samples of the data set. So your data set will be divided into different samples, and you'll be building a decision tree on each of these samples.

This way, each decision tree will be studying one subset of your data. So this way over fitting will get reduced because one decision tree is not studying the entire data set. Now let's focus on random forest. Now in order to understand random forest, we look at a small example. We can consider this data set. In this data, we have four predictor variables.

We have blood flow, blocked arteries, chest pain, and weight. Now these variables are used to predict whether or not a person has a heart disease. So we're going to use this data set to create a random forest that predicts if a person has a heart disease or not.

CREATING A RANDOM FOREST

Step 1: Create a Bootstrapped Data Set

Blood Flow	Blocked Arteries	Chest Pain	Weight	Heart Disease
Normal	Yes	Yes	195	Yes
Abnormal	No	No	130	No
Abnormal	Yes	Yes	180	Yes
Abnormal	Yes	Yes	180	Yes

Bootstrapping is an estimation method used to make predictions on a data set by re-sampling it.

Now the first step in creating a random forest is that you create a bootstrap data set. Now in bootstrapping, all you have to do is you have to randomly select samples from your original data set. Okay. And a point to note is that you can select the same sample more than once.

So, if you look at the original data set, we have a abnormal, normal, normal, and abnormal. Look at the blood flow section. Now here I've randomly selected samples, normal, abnormal, and I've selected one sample twice. You can do this in a bootstrap data set.

Now all I did here is I created a bootstrap data set. Boot strapping is nothing but an estimation method used to make predictions on a data by re-sampling the data. This is a bootstrap data set. Now even though this seems very simple, in real world problems, you'll never get such small data set.

Okay, so bootstrapping is actually a little more complex than this. Usually in real world problems, you'll have a huge data set, and bootstrapping that data set is actually a pretty complex problem. I'm here because I'm making you understand how random forest works, so that's why I've considered a small data set.

Now you're going to use the bootstrap data set that you created, and you're going to build decision trees from it. Now one more thing to note in random forest is you will not be using your entire data set. Okay, so you'll only be using few other variables at each node. So, for example, we'll only consider two variables at each step.

CREATING A RANDOM FOREST

Step 2: Creating Decision Trees

- Build a Decision Tree by using the bootstrapped data set
- Begin at the root node & choose the best attribute to split the data set
- Repeat the same process for each of the upcoming branch nodes

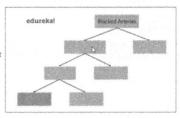

So, if you begin at the root node here, we will randomly select two variables as candidates for the root node. Okay, let's say that we selected blood flow and blocked arteries. Out of these two variables we have to select the variable that best separates the sample.

Okay. So for the sake of this example, let's say that blocked arteries is the most significant predictor, and that's why we'll assign it to the root node. Now our next step is to repeat the same process for each of these upcoming branch nodes.

CREATING A RANDOM FOREST

Step 3: Go back to Step 1 and Repeat

- Each Decision Tree predicts the output class based on the respective predictor variables used in that tree.

- Go back to step 1, create a new bootstrapped data set and then build a Decision Tree by considering only a subset of variables at each step.

- This iteration is performed 100's of times, creating multiple decision trees

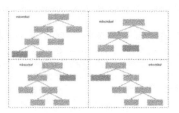

Here we'll again select two variables at random as candidates for each of these branch nodes, and then choose a variable that best separates the samples, right? So let me just repeat this entire process.

So, you know that you start creating a decision tree by selecting the root node. In random forest, you'll randomly select a couple of variables for each node, and then you'll calculate which variable best splits the data at that node.

So, for each node, we'll randomly select two or three variables. And out of those two, three variables, we'll see which variable best separates the data. Okay, so at each node, we'll because calculating information gain an entropy.

Basically, that's what I mean. At every node, you'll calculate information gain and entropy of two or three variables, and you'll see which variable has the highest information gain, and you'll keep descending downwards. That's how you create a decision tree.

So, we just created our first decision tree. Now what you

do is you'll go back to step one, and you'll repeat the entire process. So each decision tree will predict the output class based on the predictor variables that you've assigned to each decision tree.

Now let's say for this decision tree, you've assigned blood flow. Here we have blocked arteries at the root node. Here we might have blood flow at the root node and so on. So your output will depend on which predictor variable is at the root node. So each decision tree will predict the output class based on the predictor variable that you assigned in that tree.

Now what you do is you'll go back to step one, you'll create a new bootstrap data set, and then again you'll build a new decision tree. And for that decision tree, you'll consider only a subset of variables, and you'll choose the best predictor variable by calculating the information gain. So you will keep repeating this process. So you just keep repeating step two and step one.

Okay. And you'll keep creating multiple decision trees. Okay. So having a variety of decision trees in a random forest is what makes it more effective than an individual decision tree. So instead of having an individual decision tree, which is created using all the features, you can build a random forest that uses multiple decision trees wherein each decision tree has a random set of predictor variables.

CREATING A RANDOM FOREST

Step 4: Predicting the outcome of a new data point

- To predict whether a new patient has heart disease or not, run the new data down the decision trees

- After running the data down all the trees in the Random Forest, we check which class got the majority votes.

- In our case, the class 'Yes' received the most number of votes, hence it's clear that the new patient has heart disease.

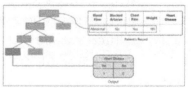

Now step number four is predicting the outcome of a new data point. So now that you've created a random forest, let's see how it can be used to predict whether a new patient has a heart disease or not. Okay, now this diagram basically has a data about the new patient. Okay, this is the data about the new patient. He doesn't have blocked arteries.

He has chest pain, and his weight is around 185 kgs. Now all you have to do is you have to run this data down each of the decision trees that you made. So, the first decision tree shows that yes, this person has heart disease. Similarly, you'll run the information of this new patient through every decision tree that you created.

CREATING A RANDOM FOREST

Step 4: Predicting the outcome of a new data point

- To predict whether a new patient has heart disease or not, run the new data down the decision trees

- After running the data down all the trees in the Random Forest, we check which class got the majority votes.

- In our case, the class 'Yes' received the most number of votes, hence it's clear that the new patient has heart disease.

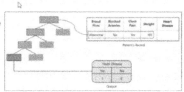

Then depending on how many votes you get for yes and no, you'll classify that patient as either having heart disease or not. All you have to do is you have to run the information of the new patient through all the decision trees that you created in the previous step, and the final output is based on the number of votes each of the class is getting.

Okay, let's say that three decision trees said that yes the patient has heart disease, and one decision tree said that no it doesn't have. So this means you will obviously classify the patient as having a heart disease because three of them voted for yes. It's based on majority.

So guys, I hope the concept behind random forest is

understandable. Now the next step is you will evaluate the efficiency of the model. Now earlier when we created the bootstrap data set we left out one entry sample. This is the entry sample we left out, because we repeated one sample twice.

If you'll remember in the bootstrap data set, here we repeated an entry twice, and we missed out on one of the entries. We missed out on one of the entries. So what we're gonna do is... So for evaluating the model, we'll be using the data entry that we missed out on.

CREATING A RANDOM FOREST

Step 5: Evaluate the Model

- In a real-world problem, about 1/3rd of the original data set is not included in the bootstrapped data set.

- This sample data set that does not include in the bootstrapped data set is known as the Out-Of-Bag (OOB) data set.

- we can measure the accuracy of a Random Forest by the proportion of OOB samples that are correctly classified.

Blood Flow	Blocked Arteries	Chest Pain	Weight	Heart Disease
Normal	No	Yes	218	No

Now in a real-world problem, about 1/3 of the original data set is not included in the bootstrap dataset. Because there's a huge amount of data in a real-world problem, so 1/3 of the original data set is not included in the bootstrap data set.

So, guys, the sample data set which is not there in your bootstrap data set is known as out-of-bag data set, because basically this is our out-of-bag data set. Now the out-of-bag data set is used to check the accuracy of the model.

Because the model was not created by using the out-of-bag data set, it will give us a good understanding of whether the model is effective or not. Now the out-of-bag data set is nothing but your testing data set. Remember, in machine learning, there's training and testing data set. So your out-of-bag data set is nothing but your testing data set.

This is used to evaluate the efficiency of your model. So

eventually, you can measure the accuracy of a random forest by the proportion of out-of-bag samples that are correctly classified, because the out-of-bag data set is used to evaluate the efficiency of your model.

So, you can calculate the accuracy by understanding how many samples or was this out-of-bag data set correctly able to classify it. So, guys, that was an explanation about how random forest works. To give you an overview, let me just run you through all the steps that we took.

So basically, this was our data set, and all we have to do is we have to predict whether a patient has heart disease or not. So, our first step was to create a bootstrap data set. A bootstrap data set is nothing but randomly selected observations from your original data set, and you can also have duplicate values in your bootstrap data set. Okay.

The next step is you're going to create a decision tree by considering a random set of predictor variables for each decision tree. Okay. So, the third step is you'll go back to step one, create a bootstrap data set. Again, create a decision tree.

So, this iteration is performed hundreds of times until you are multiple decision trees. Now that you've created a random forest, you'll use this random forest to predict the outcome. So if you're given a new data point and you have to classify it into one of the two classes, we'll just run this new information through all the decision trees.

And you'll just take the majority of the output that you're getting from the decision trees as your outcome. Now in order to evaluate the efficiency of the model, you'll use the out of the bag sample data set.

Now the out-of-bag sample is basically the sample that was not included in your bootstrap data set, but this sample is coming from your original data set, guys. This is not something that you randomly create. This data set was there in your original data set, but it was just not mentioned in your bootstrap data set.

So you'll use your out-of-bag sample in order to calculate the accuracy of your random forest. So the proportion of out-of-bag samples that are correctly classified will give you the accuracy of your model. So that is all for random forest.

So, guys, I'll discuss other classification algorithms with you, and only then I'll show you a demo on the classification algorithms. Now our next algorithm is something known as naive Bayes.

NAIVE BAYES

Naive Bayes is, again, a supervised classification algorithm, which is based on the Bayes Theorem. Now the Bayes Theorem basically follows a probabilistic approach. The main idea behind naive Bayes is that the predictor variables in a machine learning model are independent of each other, meaning that the outcome of a model depends on a set of independent variables that have nothing to do with each other.

NAÏVE BAYES

- Naïve Bayes is based on the Bayes Theorem that is used to solve classification problems by following a probabilistic approach.

- It is based on the idea that the predictor variables in a Machine Learning model are independent of each other.

- P(A|B): Conditional probability of event A occurring, given the event B

- P(A): Probability of event A occurring

- P(B): Probability of event B occurring

- P(B|A): Conditional probability of event B occurring, given the event A

$$P(A|B) = \frac{P(B|A)P(A)}{P(B)}$$

Now a lot of you might ask why is naive Bayes called naive. Now usually, when I tell anybody why naive Bayes, they keep asking me why is naive Bayes called naive. So in real world problems predictor variables aren't always independent of each other.

There is always some correlation between the independent variables. Now because naive Bayes considers each predictor variable to be independent of any other variable in the model, it is called naive. This is an assumption that naive Bayes states. Now let's understand the math behind the naive Bayes algorithm.

So like I mentioned, the principle behind naive Bayes is

the Bayes Theorem, which is also known as the Bayes Rule. The Bayes Theorem is used to calculate the conditional probability, which is nothing but the probability of an event occurring based on information about the events in the past.

This is the mathematical equation for the Bayes Theorem. Now, in this equation, the LHS is nothing but the conditional probability of event A occurring, given the event B. P of A is nothing but probability of event A occurring P of B is probability of event B.

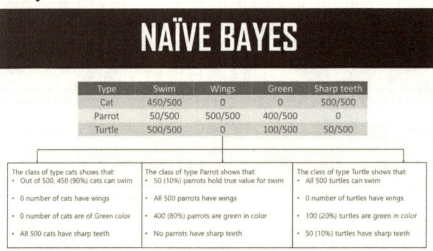

NAÏVE BAYES

Type	Swim	Wings	Green	Sharp teeth
Cat	450/500	0	0	500/500
Parrot	50/500	500/500	400/500	0
Turtle	500/500	0	100/500	50/500

the class of type cats shows that:	The class of type Parrot shows that:	The class of type Turtle shows that:
• Out of 500, 450 (90%) cats can swim	• 50 (10%) parrots hold true value for swim	• All 500 turtles can swim
• 0 number of cats have wings	• All 500 parrots have wings	• 0 number of turtles have wings
• 0 number of cats are of Green color	• 400 (80%) parrots are green in color	• 100 (20%) turtles are green in color
• All 500 cats have sharp teeth	• No parrots have sharp teeth	• 50 (10%) turtles have sharp teeth

And PB of A is nothing but the conditional probability of event B occurring, given the event A. Now let's try to understand how naive Bayes works. Now consider this data set of around thousand 500 observations. Okay, here we have the following output classes.

NAÏVE BAYES

To predict whether the animal is a Cat, Parrot or a Turtle based on the defined predictor variables (swim, wings, green, sharp teeth).

	Swim	Wings	Green	Sharp Teeth
Observation	True	False	True	False

To solve this, we will use the Naïve Bayes approach:

$$P(H|Multiple\ Evidences) = P(C1|H) * P(C2|H) ...... * P(Cn|H) * P(H) / P(Multiple\ Evidences)$$

We have either cat, parrot, or turtle. These are our output classes, and the predictor variables are swim, wings, green colour, and sharp teeth. Okay. So, basically, your type is your output variable, and swim, wings, green, and sharp teeth are your predictor variables.

Your output variables have three classes, cat, parrot, and turtle. Okay. Now I've summarized this table I've shown on the screen. The first thing you can see is the class of type cats shows that out of 500 cats, 450 can swim, meaning that 90% of them can.

And zero number of cats have wings, and zero number of cats are green in colour, and 500 out of 500 cats have sharp teeth. Okay. Now, coming to parrot, it says 50 out of 500 parrots have true value for swim. Now guys, obviously, this does not hold true in real world.

NAÏVE BAYES

In the observation, the variables Swim and Green are true and the outcome can be any one of the animals (Cat, Parrot, Turtle).

$$P(H|Multiple\ Evidences) = P(C1|H) * P(C2|H) ......*P(Cn|H) * P(H) / P(Multiple\ Evidences)$$

To check if the animal is a cat:
$P(Cat | Swim, Green) = P(Swim|Cat) * P(Green|Cat) * P(Cat) / P(Swim, Green)$
$= 0.9 * 0 * 0.333 / P(Swim, Green) = 0$

I don't think there are any parrots who can swim, but I've just created this data set so that we can understand naive Bayes. So, meaning that 10% of parrots have true value for swim. Now all 500 parrots have wings, and 400 out of 500 parrots are green in colour, and zero parrots have sharp teeth.

Coming to the turtle class, all 500 turtles can swim. Zero number of turtles have wings. And out of 500, hundred turtles are green in colour, meaning that 20% of the turtles are green in colour. And 50 out of 500 turtles have sharp teeth. So that's what we understand from this data set.

Now the problem here is we are given our observation over here, given some value for swim, wings, green, and sharp teeth. What we need to do is we need to predict whether the animal is a cat, parrot, or a turtle, based on these values. So the goal here to predict whether it is a cat, parrot, or a turtle based on all these defined parameters. Okay.

Based on the value of swim, wings, green, and sharp teeth, we'll understand whether the animal is a cat, or is it a parrot, or is it a turtle. So, if you look at the observation, the variables swim and green have a value of true, and the outcome can be anyone of the types.

It can either be a cat, it can be a parrot, or it can be a turtle. So in order to check if the animal is a cat, all you have to do is you have to calculate the conditional probability at each step. So here what we're doing is we need to calculate the probability that this is a cat, given that it can swim and it is green in colour.

First, we'll calculate the probability that it can swim, given that it's a cat. And two, the probability that it is green and the probability of it being green, given that it is a cat, and then we'll multiply it with the probability of it being a cat divided by the probability of swim and green. Okay. So, guys, I know you all can calculate the probability.

It's quite simple. So once you calculate the probability here, you'll get a direct value of zero. Okay, you'll get a value of zero, meaning that this animal is definitely not a cat. Similarly, if you do this for parrots, you calculate a conditional probability, you'll get a value of 0.0264 divided by probability of swim comma green.

We don't know this probability. Similarly, if you check this for the turtle, you'll get a probability of 0.066 divided by P swim comma green. Okay. Now for these calculations, the denominator is the same. The value of the denominator is the same, and the value of and the probability of it being a turtle is greater than that of a parrot.

So that's how we can correctly predict that the animal is actually a turtle. So guys, this is how naive Bayes works. You basically calculate the conditional probability at each step. Whatever classification needs to be done, that has to be calculated through probability. There's a lot of statistic that comes into naive Bayes.

And if you all want to learn more about statistics and probability, I'll leave a link in the end of the book. You all can watch that video as well for reference. There I've explain exactly what conditional probability is, and the Bayes Theorem is also explained very well.

NAÏVE BAYES

In the observation, the variables Swim and Green are true and the outcome can be any one of the animals (Cat, Parrot, Turtle).

$$P(H|Multiple\ Evidences) = P(C1|H) * P(C2|H) ......*P(Cn|H) * P(H) / P(Multiple\ Evidences)$$

To check if the animal is a Parrot:
$P(Parrot|Swim,\ Green) = P(Swim|Parrot) * P(Green|Parrot) * P(Parrot) / P(Swim,\ Green)$
$= 0.1 * 0.80 * 0.333 / P(Swim,\ Green)$
$= 0.0264 / P(Swim,\ Green)$

So, you all can check out that video link in the end of the book also. And apart from this, if you all have any doubts regarding any of the algorithms, please leave them in the comment section. Okay, I'll solve your doubts. And apart from that, I'll also leave a couple of links for each of the algorithms in the end of the book.

Because if you want more in-depth understanding of each of the algorithms, you can check out that content. Since this is a full course book, I have to cover all the topics, and it is hard for me to make you understand in-depth of each topic.

So, I'll leave a couple of links in the end of the book for your reference. You can watch those videos as well. Make sure you checkout the probability and statistics video. So now let's move on and locate our next algorithm, which is the K nearest neighbour algorithm.

K NEAREST NEIGHBOUR (KNN)

Now KNN, which basically stands for K nearest neighbour, is, again, a supervised classification algorithm that classifies a new data point into the target class or the output class, depending on the features of its neighbouring data points. That's why it's called K nearest neighbour. So, let's try to understand KNN with a small analogy.

let's say that we want a machine to distinguish between the images of cats and dogs. So to do this, we must input our data set of cat and dog images, and we have to train our model to detect the animal based on certain features. For example, features such as pointy ears can be used to identify cats. Similarly, we can identify dogs based on their long ears.

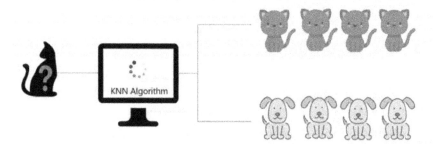

K Nearest Neighbour is a Supervised Learning algorithm that classifies a new data point into the target class, depending on the features of it's neighbouring data points.

So, after starting the data set during the training phase, when a new image is given to the model, the KNN algorithm will classify it into either cats or dogs, depending on the similarity in their features.

Okay, let's say that a new image has pointy ears, it will classify that image as cat, because it is similar to the cat images, because it's similar to its neighbours. In this manner, the KNN algorithm classifies the data point based on how similar they are to their neighbouring data points. So this is a small example. We'll discuss more about it in the further slides.

Now let me tell you a couple of features of KNN algorithm. So, first of all, we know that it is a supervised learning algorithm. It uses labelled input data set to predict the output of the data points. Then it is also one of the simplest machine learning algorithms, and it can be easily implemented for a varied set of problems.

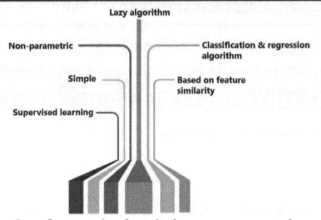

Another feature is that it is non-parametric, meaning that it does not take in any assumptions. For example, naive Bayes is a parametric model, because it assumes that all the independent variables are in no way related to each other.

It has assumptions about the model. K nearest neighbour has no such assumptions. That's why it's considered a non-parametric model. Another feature is that it is a lazy algorithm. Now, lazy algorithm basically is any algorithm that memorizes the training set, instead of learning a discriminative function from the training data.

Now, even though KNN is mainly a classification algorithm, it can also be used for regression cases. So KNN is actually both a classification and a regression algorithm. But mostly, you'll see that it'll be used on the four classification problems.

The most important feature about a K nearest neighbour is that it's based on feature similarity with its neighbouring data points. You'll understand this in the example that I'm gonna tell you. Now, in this image, we have two classes of data.

We have class A which is squares and class B which are triangles. Now the problem statement is to assign the new input data point to one of the two classes by using the KNN algorithm.

So the first step in the KNN algorithm is to define the value of K. But what is the K in the KNN algorithm stand for? Now the K stands for the number of nearest neighbours, and that's why it's got the name K nearest neighbours.

K NEAREST NEIGHBOUR (KNN)

Here k=7, find the 7 nearest neighbours

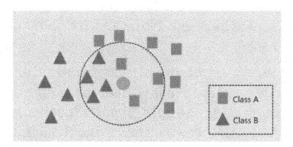

Now, in this image, I've defined the value of K as three. This means that the algorithm will consider the three neighbours that are closest to the new data point in order to decide the class of the new data point.

So the closest between the data point is calculated by using measure such as Euclidean distance and Manhattan distance, which I'll be explaining in a while. So our K is equal to three. The neighbours include two squares and one triangle.

If I were to classify the new data point based on K equal to three, then it should be assigned to class A, correct? It should be assigned to squares. But what if the K value is set to seven. Here I'm basically telling my algorithm to look for the seven nearest neighbours and classify the new data point into the class it is most similar to. So, our K equal to seven.

The neighbours include three squares and four triangles. So if I were to classify the new data point based on K equal to seven, then it would be assigned to class B, since majority of its neighbours are from class B.

Now this is where a lot of us get confused. So how do we know which K values is the most suitable for K nearest neighbour. Now there are a couple methods used to calculate the K value. One of them is known as the elbow method.

We'll be discussing the elbow method in the upcoming slides. So for now let me just show you the measures that are involved behind KNN. Okay, there's very simple math behind the K nearest neighbour algorithm. So I'll be discussing the Euclidean distance with you. Now in this figure, we have to measure the distance between P one and P two by using Euclidean distance.

I'm sure a lot of you already know what Euclidean distance is. It is something that we learned in eighth or 10th grade. I'm not sure. So all you're doing is you're extracting X one. So the formula is basically x two minus x one the whole square plus y two minus y one the whole square, and the root of that is the Euclidean distance. It's as simple as that.

EUCLIDEAN DISTANCE

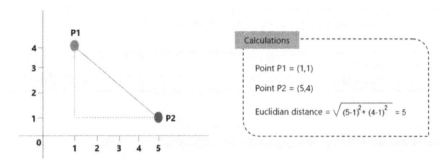

So Euclidean distance is used as a measure to check the closeness of data points. So basically, KNN uses the Euclidean distance to check the closeness of a new data point with its neighbours. So guys, it's as simple as that. KNN makes use of simple measures in order to solve very complex problems. Okay, and this is one of the reasons why KNN is such a commonly used algorithm. Coming to support vector machine. Now, this is our last algorithm under classification algorithms.

SUPPORT VECTOR MACHINE (SVM)

Now guys, don't get paranoid because of the name. Support vector machine actually is one of the simplest algorithms in supervised learning. Okay, it is basically used to classify data into different classes. It's a classification algorithm.

SUPPORT VECTOR MACHINE (SVM)

Support Vector Machine (SVM) is a supervised classification method that separates data using hyperplanes.

Supervised machine learning algorithm

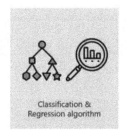

Classification & Regression algorithm

SVM kernel functions

Now unlike most algorithms, SVM makes use of something known as a hyperplane which acts like a decision boundary between the separate classes. Okay. Now SVM can be used to generate multiple separating hyperplanes, such that the data is divided into segments, and each segment contains only one kind of data.

So, a few features of SVM include that it is a supervised learning algorithm, meaning that it's going to study a labelled training data. Another feature is that it is again a regression and a classification algorithm.

Even though SVM is mainly used for classification, there is something known as the support vector regressor. That is useful regression problems. Now, SVM can also be used to classify non-linear data by using kernel tricks. Non-linear data is basically data that cannot be separated by using a single linear line. I'll be talking more about this in the upcoming slides.

SUPPORT VECTOR MACHINE (SVM)

Support Vector Machine (SVM) is a supervised classification method that separates data using hyperplanes.

Now let's move on and discuss how SVM works. Now again, in order to make you understand how support vector machine works, you look at a small scenario. For a second, pretend that you own a farm and you have a problem. You need to set up a fence to protect your rabbits from a pack of wolves.

Okay, now, you need to decide where you want to build your fence. So, one way to solve the problem is by using support vector machines. So, if I do that and if I try to draw a decision boundary between the rabbits and the wolves, it looks something like this. Now you can clearly build a fence along this line.

SUPPORT VECTOR MACHINE (SVM)

Support Vector Machine (SVM) is a supervised classification method that separates data using hyperplanes.

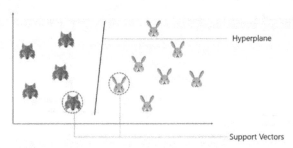

So in simple terms, this is exactly how your support vector machines work. It draws a decision boundary, which is nothing but a hyperplane between any two classes in order to separate them or classify them. Now I know that you're thinking how do you know where to draw a hyperplane.

The basic principle behind SVM is to draw a hyperplane that best separates the two classes. In our case, the two classes are the rabbits and the wolves. Now before we move any further, let's discuss the different terminologies that are there in support vector machine. So that is basically a hyperplane. It is a decision boundary that best separates the two classes. Now, support vectors, what exactly are support vectors.

So when you start with the support vector machine, you start by drawing a random hyperplane. And then you check the distance between the hyperplane and the closest data point from each of the class. These closest data points to the hyperplane are known as support vectors. Now these two data points are the closest to your hyperplane.

So these are known as support vectors, and that's where the name comes from, support vector machines. Now the hyperplane is drawn based on these support vectors. And optimum hyperplane will be the one which has a maximum distance from each of the support vectors, meaning that the distance between the hyperplane and the support vectors has to be maximum.

SUPPORT VECTOR MACHINE (SVM)

Support Vector Machine (SVM) is a supervised classification method that separates data using hyperplanes.

So, to sum it up, SVM is used to classify data by using a hyperplane, such that the distance between the hyperplane and the support vector is maximum. Now this distance is nothing but the margin. Now let's try to solve a problem.

Let's say that I input a new data point and I want to draw a hyperplane such that it best separates these two classes. So what do I do? I start out by drawing a hyperplane, and then I check the distance between the hyperplane and the support vectors. So, basically here, I'm trying to check if the margin is maximum for this hyperplane. But what if I drew the hyperplane like this? The margin for this hyperplane is clearly being more than the previous one.

INTRODUCTION TO NON-LINEAR SVM

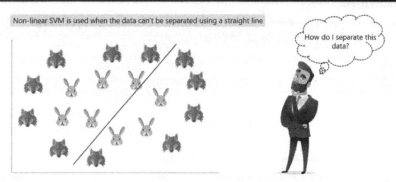

Non-linear SVM is used when the data can't be separated using a straight line

How do I separate this data?

So this is my optimal hyperplane. This is exactly how you understand which hyperplane needs to be chosen, because you can draw multiple hyperplanes. Now, the best hyperplane is the one that has a maximum module. So, this is my optimal hyperplane. Now so far it was quite easy. Our data was linearly separable, which means that you could draw a straight line to separate the two classes.

But what will you do if the data looks like this? You possibly cannot draw a hyperplane like this. You possibly cannot draw a hyperplane like this. It doesn't separate the two classes. We can clearly see rabbits and wolves in both of the classes. Now this is exactly where non-linear SVM comes into the picture. Okay, this is what the kernel trick is all about.

Now, kernel is basically something that can be used to transform data into another dimension that has a clear dividing margin between classes of data. So, basically the kernel function offers the user the option of transforming non-linear spaces into linear ones. Until this point, if you notice that we were plotting our data on two-dimensional space.

INTRODUCTION TO NON-LINEAR SVM

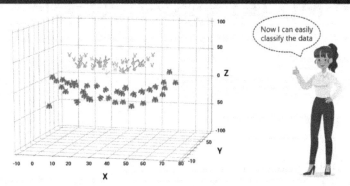

We had x and y-axis. A simple trick is transforming the two variables, x and y, into a new feature space, which involves a new variable z. So, basically, what we're doing is we're visualizing the data on a three-dimensional space. So, when you transform the 2D space into a 3D space, you can clearly see a dividing margin between the two classes of data.

You can clearly draw a line in the middle that separates these two data sets. So, guys, this sums up the whole idea behind support vector machines. Support vector machines are very easy to understand. Now, this was all for our supervised learning algorithms. Now, before I move on to unsupervised learning algorithms,

DEMO (CLASSIFICATION ALGORITHMS)

I'll be running a demo. We'll be running a demo in order to understand all the classification algorithms that we studied so far. Earlier in the session, we ran a demo for the regression algorithms.

Now we'll run for the classification algorithms. So, enough of theory. Let's open up Python, and let's start looking at how these classification algorithms work. Now, here what we'll be doing is we'll implement multiple classification algorithms by using the scikit-learn.

Okay, it's one of the most popular machine learning tools for Python. Now we'll be using a simple data set for the task of training a classifier to distinguish between the different types of fruits. The purpose of this demo is to implement multiple classification algorithms for the same set of problem. So as usual, you start by importing all your libraries in Python.

Again, guys, if you don't know Python, check the end of

the book, I'll leave a link their end of the book. You can go through that video as well. Next, what we're doing is we're reading the fruit data in the form of table. You stored it in a variable called fruits.

Now if you wanna see the first few rows of the data, let's print the first few observations in our data set. So, this is our data set. These are the fruit labels. So we have around four fruits in our data set. We have apple, we have mandarin, orange, and lemon.

Okay. Now, fruit label denotes nothing but the label of apple, which is one. Mandarin has two. Similarly, orange is labelled as three. And lemon is labelled as four. Then a fruit subtype is basically the family of fruit it belongs to. Mass is the mass of the fruit, width, height, and colour score. These are all our predictor variables.

We have to identify the type of fruit, depending on these predictor variables. So, first, we saw a couple of observations over here. Next, if you want to see the shape of your data set, this is what it looks like. There are around 59 observations with seven predictor variables, which is one, two, three, four, five, six, and seven.

We have seven variables in total. Sorry, not predictor variables. This seven denotes both your predictor and your target variable. Next, I'm just showing you the four fruits that we have in our data set, which is apple, mandarin, orange, and lemon. Next, I'm just grouping fruits by their names. Okay. So we have 19 apples in our data set. We have 16 lemons.

We have only five mandarins, and we have 19 oranges. Even though the number of mandarin samples is low, we'll have to work with it, because right now I'm just trying to make you understand the classification algorithms. The main aim for me behind doing these demos is so that you understand how classification algorithms work.

Now what you can do is you can also plot a graph in order to see the frequency of each of these fruits. Okay, I'll show you what the plot looks like. The number of apples and oranges is the same. We have I think around 19 apples and oranges.

And similarly, this is the count for lemons. Okay. So this is a small visualization. Guys, visualization is actually very important when it comes to machine learning, because you can see most of the relations and correlations by plotting graphs. You can't see those correlations by just running code and all of that.

Only when you plot different variables on your graph, you'll understand how they are related. One of the main task in machine learning is to visualize data. It ensures that you understand the correlation between data. Next, what we're gonna do is we'll graph something known as a box plot.

Okay, a box plot basically helps you understand the distribution of your data. Let me run the box plot, and I'll show you what exactly I mean. So this is our box plot. So, box plot will basically give you a clearer idea of the distribution of your input variables.

It is mainly used in exploratory data analysis, and it represents the distribution of the data and its variability. Now, the box plot contains upper quartile and lower quartile. So the box plot basically spanned your interquartile range or something known as IQR.

IQR is nothing but your third quartile subtracted from your first quartile. Now again, this involves statistics and probability. So I'll be leaving a link in the end of the book. You can go through that video. I've explained statistics probability, IQR, range, and all of that in there.

So, one of the main reasons why box plots are used is to

detect any sort of outliers in the data. Since the box plot spans the IQR, it detects the data point that lie outside the average range.

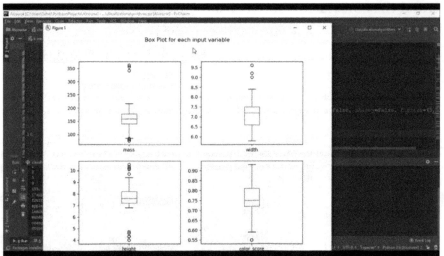

So if you see in the coloured space, most of the data is distributed around the IQR, whereas here the data are not that well distributed. Height also is not very well distributed, but colour space is pretty well distributed. This is what the box plot shows you.

So guys, this involves a lot of math. All of these, each and every function in machine learning involves a lot of math. So you know it's necessary to have a good understanding of statistics, probability, and all of that. Now, next, what we'll do is we'll plot a histogram.

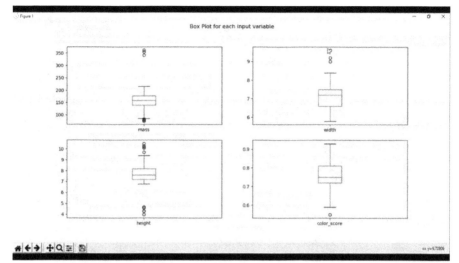

Histogram will basically show you the frequency of occurrence. Let me just plot this, and then we'll try and understand. So here you can understand a few correlations. Okay, some pairs of these attributes are correlated. For example, mass and width, they're somehow correlated along the same ranges.

So this suggests a high correlation and a predictable relationship. Like if you look at the graphs, they're quite similar. So for each of the predictor variables, I've drawn a histogram. For each of that input data, we've drawn a histogram.

Now guys, again, like I said, plotting graphs is very important because you understand a lot of correlations that you cannot understand by just looking at your data, or just running operations on your data. Repeat, or just running code on your data.

Okay. Now, next, what we're doing here is we're just dividing the data set into target and predictor variables. So, basically, I've created an array of feature names which has your predictor variables.

It has mass, width, height, colour space. And you have assigned that as X, since this is your input, and y is your output which is your fruit label. That'll show whether it is an apple, orange, lemon, and so on. Now, the next step that we'll perform over here is pretty evident.

Again, this is data splicing. So data splicing, by now, I'm sure all of you know what it is. It is splitting your data into training and testing data. So that's what we've done over here. Next, we're importing something known as the MinMaxScaler.

Scaling or normalizing your data is very important in machine learning. Now, I'm seeing this because your raw data can be very biased. So it's very important to normalize your data. Now when I say normalize your data, so if you look at the value of mass and if you look at the value of height and colour, you see that mass is ranging in hundreds and double digits, whereas height is in single digit, and colour score is not even in single digits.

130

So, if some of your variables have a very high range, you know they have a very high scale, like they're in two digits or three digits, whereas other variables are single digits and lesser, then your output is going to be very biased. It's obvious that it's gonna be very biased.

That's why you have to scale your data in such a way that all of these values will have a similar range. So that's exactly what the scaler function does. Okay. Now since we have already divided our data into training and testing data, our next step is to build the model.

So, first, we're gonna be using the logistic regression algorithm. I've already discussed logistic regression with you all. It's a classification algorithm, which is basically used to predict the outcome of a categorical variable.

So we already have the logistic regression class in Python. All you have to do is you have to give an instance for this function, which is logger over here. And I'm fitting this instance with a training data set, meaning that I'm running the algorithm with the training data set.

Once you do that, you can calculate the accuracy by using this function. So here I'm calculate the accuracy on the training data set and on the testing data set. Okay, so let's look at the output of this. Now guys, ignore this future warning. Warnings are ignored in Python. Now, accuracy of the logistic regression classifier on the training data set is around 70%.

It was pretty good on the training data set. But when it comes to classifying on the test data set, it's only 40%, which is not that good for a classifier. Now again, this can depend on the problem statement, for which problem statement is logistic regression more suitable.

Next, we'll do the same thing using the decision tree. So again, we just call the decision tree function, and we'll fit it with the training data set, and we'll calculate the accuracy of the decision tree on the training, and the testing data set. So if you do that for a decision tree on the training data set, you get 100% accuracy. But on the testing data set, you have around 87% of accuracy.

This is something that I discussed with you all earlier, that this is decision trees are very good with training data set, because of a process known as overfitting. But when it comes to classifying the outcome on the testing data set, the accuracy reduces. Now, this is very good compared to logistic regression.

For this problem statement, decision trees work better that logistic regression. Coming to KNN classifier. Again, all you have to do is you have to call the K neighbour classifier, this function. And you have to fit this with the training data set.

If you calculate the accuracy for a KNN classifier, we get a good accuracy actually. On the training data set, we get an accuracy of 95%. And on the testing data set, it's 100%. That is really good, because our testing data set actually achieved more of an accuracy than on a training data set.

Now all of this depends on the value of K that you've chosen for KNN. Now, I mentioned that you use the elbow method to choose the K value in the K nearest neighbour. I'll be discussing the elbow method in the next section. So, don't worry if you haven't understood that yet. Now, we're also using a naive Bayes classifier. Here we're using a Gaussian naive Bayes classifier.

Gaussian is basically a type of naive Bayes classifier. I'm not going to go into depth of this, because it'll just extend our session too much longer. Okay. And if you want to know more about this, I'll leave a link in the description box. You can read all about the caution naive Bayes classifier.

Now, the math behind this is the same. It uses naive Bayes; it uses the Bayes Theorem itself. Now again, we're gonna call this class, and then we're going to run our data, training data on it. So using the naive Bayes classifier, we're getting an accuracy of 0.86 on the training data set.

And on the testing data set, we're getting 67% accuracy. Okay. Now let's do the same thing with support vector machines. Importing the support vector classifier. And we are fitting the training data into the algorithm. We're getting an accuracy of around 61% on the training data set and 33% on the testing data set. Now guys, this accuracy and all depends also on the problem statement.

It depends on the type of data that support vector machines get. Usually, SVM is very good on large data sets. Now since we have a very small data set over here, it's sort of obvious by the accuracy, so less. So guys, these were a couple of classification algorithms that I showed you here. Now, because our KNN classifier classified our data set more accurately we'll look at the predictions that the KNN classifier mean.

Okay Now we're storing all our predicted values in the predict variable. now in order to show you the accuracy of the KNN model, we're going to us something known as the confusion matrix. So, a confusion matrix is a table that is often used to describe the performance of a classification model.

So, confusion matrix actually represents a tabular representation of actual versus predicted values. So when you draw a confusion matrix on the actual versus predicted values for the KNN classifier, this is what the confusion matrix looks like. Now, we have four rows over here. If you see, we have four rows.

The first row represents apples, second, mandarin, third

represents lemons, and fourth, oranges. So this four value corresponds to zero comma zero, meaning that it was correctly able to classify all the four apples. Okay. This one value represents one comma one, meaning that our classifier correctly classified this as mandarins.

This matrix is drawn on actual values versus predicted values. Now, if you look at the summary of the confusion matrix, we'll get something known as precision recall, f1-score and support. Precision is basically the ratio of the correctly predicted positive observations to the total predicted positive observations.

So the correctly predicted positive observations are four, and there are total of four apples in the testing data set. So that's where I get a precision of one. Okay. Recall on the other hand is the ratio of correctly predicted positive observations to all the observations in the class.

Again, we've correctly classified four apples, and there are a total of four apples. F1-score is nothing but the weighted average of your precision and your recall. Okay, and your support basically denotes the number of data points that were correctly classified. So, in our KNN algorithm, since we got 100% accuracy, all our data points were correctly classified.

So, 15 out of 15 were correctly classified because we have 100% accuracy. So that's how you read a confusion matrix. Okay, you have four important measures, precision, recall, f1-score, and support. F1-score is just the ratio or the weighted average of your precision and your recall.

So precision is basically the correctly predicted positive observations to the total predicted positive observations. Recall is a ratio of the predicted positive observations to all your observations. So guys, that was it for the demo of classification algorithms, we discuss regression algorithms and we discussed classification algorithms. Now it's time to talk about unsupervised learning algorithms.

UNSUPERVISED LEARNING ALGORITHMS

Under unsupervised learning algorithms may try to solve clustering problems. And the most important clustering algorithm there is, known as K-means clustering.

K-MEANS CLUSTERING

So we're going to discuss the K-means algorithm, and also show you a demo where we'll be executing the clustering algorithm, and you're seeing how it implemented to solve a problem. Now, the main aim of the K-means algorithm is to group similar elements or data points into a cluster.

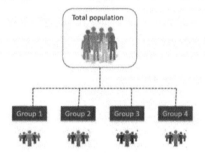

K-MEANS CLUSTERING

The process by which objects are classified into a predefined number of groups so that they are as much dissimilar as possible from one group to another group, but as much similar as possible within each group.

So it is basically the process by which objects are classified interest a predefined number of groups, so that they are much dissimilar as possible from one group to another group, but as much similar as possible within each group.

Now what I mean is let's say you're trying to cluster this population into four different groups, such that each group has people within a specified range of age. Let's say group one is of people between the age 18 and 22. Similarly, group two is between 23 and 35. Group three is 36 and 39 or something like that.

So let's say you're trying to cluster people into different groups based on their age. So for such problems, you can make use of the K-means clustering algorithm. One of the major applications of the clustering algorithm is seen in targeted marketing. I don't know how many of you are aware of targeted marketing.

Targeted marketing is all about marketing a specific product to a specific audience. Let's say you're trying to sell fancy clothes or a fancy set of bags and all of that. And the perfect audience for such product would be teenagers. It would be people around the age of 16 to 21 or 18.

So that is what target marketing is all about. Your product is marketed to a specific audience that might be interested in it. That is what targeted marketing is. So K means clustering is use majorly in targeted marketing.

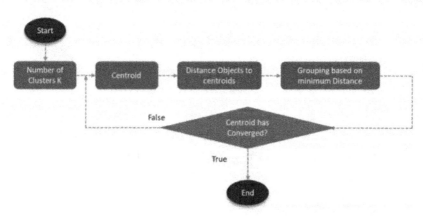

A lot of eCommerce websites like Amazon, Flipkart, eBay. All of these make use of clustering algorithms in order to target the right audience. Now let's see how the K-means clustering works. Now the K in K-means denotes the number of clusters.

Let's say I give you a data set containing 20 points, and you want to cluster this data set into four clusters. That means your K will be equal to four. So K basically stands for the number of clusters in your data set, or the number of clusters you want to form. You start by defining the number K. Now for each of these clusters, you're going to choose a centroid.

So, for every cluster, there are four cluster in our data set. For each of these clusters, you'll randomly select one of the data points as a centroid. Now what you'll do is you'll start computing the distance from that centroid to every other point in that cluster.

As you keep computing the centroid and the distance between the centroid and other data points in that cluster, your centroid keeps shifting, because you're trying to get to the average of that cluster. Whenever you're trying to get to the average of the cluster, the centroid keeps shifting, because the centroid keeps converging and it keeps shifting.

Let's try to understand how K-means works. Let's say that this data set, this is given to us. Let's say if you're given random points like these and you're asked to us K-means algorithm on this. So your first step will be to decide the number of clusters you want to create. So let's say I wanna create three different clusters. So my K value will be equal to three.

The next step will be to provide centroids of all the clusters. What you'll do is initially you'll randomly pick three data points as your centroids for your three different clusters. So basically, this red denotes the centroid for one cluster.

Blue denotes a centroid for another cluster. And this green dot denotes the centroid for another cluster. Now what happens in K-means, the algorithm will calculate the Euclidean distance of the points from each centroid and assign the points to the closest cluster. Now since we had three centroids here, now what you're gonna do is you're going to calculate the distance from each and every data point to all the centroids, and you're going to check which data point is closest to which centroid.

So let's say your data point A is closest to the blue centroid. So you're going to assign the data point A to the blue cluster. So based on the distance between the centroid and the cluster, you're going to form three different clusters.

Now again, you're going to calculate the centroid and you're going to form a new cluster which is from better clusters, because you're recomputing all those centroids. Basically, your centroids represent the mean of each of your cluster. So you need to make sure that your mean is actually the centroid of each cluster. So you'll keep recomputing this centroids until the position of your centroid does not change.

That means that your centroid is actually the main or the average of that particular cluster. So that's how K-means works. It's very simple. All you have to do is you have to start by defining the K value. After that, you have to randomly pick the number of case centroids.

K-MEANS CLUSTERING

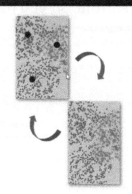

1. First we need to decide the number of clusters to be made. (Guessing)
2. Then we provide centroids of all the clusters. (Guessing)
3. The Algorithm calculates Euclidian distance of the points from each centroid and assigns the point to the closest cluster.
4. Next the Centroids are calculated again, when we have our new cluster.
5. The distance of the points from the centre of clusters are calculated again and points are assigned to the closest cluster.
6. And then again the new centroid for the cluster is calculated.
7. These steps are repeated until we have a repetition in centroids or new centroids are very close to the previous ones.

Then you're going to calculate the average distance of each of the data points from the centroids, and you're going to assign a data point to the centroid it is closest to. That's how K-means works. It's a very simple process.

All you have to do is us have to keep iterating, and you have to recompute the centroid value until the centroid value does not change, until you get a constant centroid value. Now guys, again, in K-means, you make use of distance measures like Euclidean.

I've already discussed what Euclidean is all about. So, to summarize how K-means works, you start by picking the number of clusters. Then you pick a centroid. After that, you calculate the distance of the objects to the centroid.

Then you group the data points into specific clusters based on their distance. You have to keep computing the centroid until each data point is assigned to the closest cluster, so that's how K-means works. Now let's look at the elbow method.

The elbow method is basically used in order to find out the most optimum k value for a particular problem. So the elbow method is quite simple actually. You start off by computing the sum of squared errors for some values of K.

Now sum of squared error is basically the sum of the squared distance between each member of the cluster and its centroid. So you basically calculate the sum of squared errors for different values of K. For example, you can consider K value as two, four, six, eight, 10, 12. Consider all these values, compute the sum of squared errors for each of these values.

K-MEANS CLUSTERING

The Elbow Method:

First of all, compute the sum of squared error (SSE) for some values of k (for example 2, 4, 6, 8, etc.). The SSE is defined as the sum of the squared distance between each member of the cluster and its centroid. Mathematically:

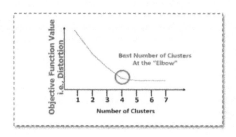

$$SSE = \sum_{i=1}^{K} \sum_{x \in c_i} dist(x, c_i)^2$$

Now if you plot your K value against your sum of squared errors, you will see that the error decreases as K gets larger. This is because the number of clusters increase. If the number of clusters increases, it means that the distortion gets smaller.

The distortion keeps decreasing as the number of clusters increase. That's because the more clusters you have, the closer each centroid will be with its data points. So as you keep increasing the number of clusters, your distortion will also decrease.

So, the idea of the elbow method is to choose the K at which the distortion decreases abruptly. So, if you look at this graph at K equal to four, the distortion is abruptly decreasing. So, this is how you find the value of K. When your distortion drops abruptly, that is the most optimal K value you should be choosing for your problem statement.

So, let me repeat the idea behind the elbow method. You're just going to graph the number of clusters you have versus the squared sum of errors. This graph will basically give you the distortion. Now the distortion obviously going to decrease if you increase the number of clusters, and there is gonna be one point in this graph wherein the distortion decreases very abruptly.

Now for that point, you need to find out the value of K, and that'll be your most optimal K value. That's how you choose your K-means K value and your KNN K value as well. So guys, this is how the elbow method is. It's very simple and it can be easily implemented.

DEMO (UNSUPERVISED LEARNING)

Now we're gonna look at a small demo which involves K-means. This is actually a very interesting demo. Now guys, one interesting application of clustering is in colour compression with images.

For example, imagine you have an image with millions of colours in it. In most images, a large number of colours will be unused, and many of the pixels in the image will have similar or even identical colours. Now having too many colours in your image makes it very hard for image processing an image analysis.

So, this is one area where K-means is applied very often. It's applied in image segmentation, image analysis, image compression, and so on. So, what we're gonna do in this demo is we are going to use an image from the scikit-learn data set. Okay, it is a prebuilt image, and you will require to install the pillow package for this.

We're going to use an image form the scikit-learn data set module. So we'll begin by importing the libraries as usual, and we'll be loading our image as china. The image is china.jpg, and we'll be loading this in a variable called china.

So, if you wanna look at the shape of our image, you can run this command. So we're gonna get a three-dimensional value. So, we're getting 427 comma 640 comma three. Now this is basically a three-dimensional array of size, height, width, and RGB. It contains red, blue, green contributions, as integers from zero to 255.

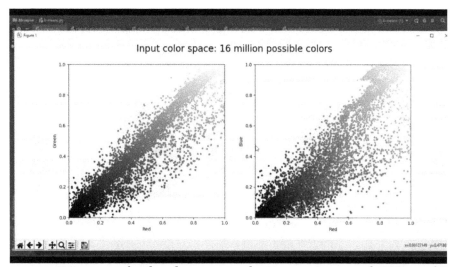

So, your pixel values range between zero and 255, and I think zero stands for your black, and 255 represents white if I'm not wrong. And basically, that's what this array shape denotes. Now one way we can view this set of pixels is as a cloud of points in a three-dimensional colour space.

So what we'll do is we will reshape the data and rescale the colour, so that they lie between zero and one. So the output of this will be a two dimensional array now. So basically, we can visualize these pixels in this colour space.

Now what we're gonna do is we're gonna try and plot our pixels. We have a really huge data set which contains around 16 million possible colours. So this denotes a very, very large data set. So, let me show you what it looks like. We have red against green and red against blue. These are our RGB value, and we can have around 16 million possible combination of colours.

The data set is way too large or us to compute. So what we'll do is we will reduce these 16 million colours to just 16 colours. We can do that by using K-means clustering, because we can cluster similar colours into similar groups. So this is exactly where we'll be importing K-means. Now, one thing to note here is because we're dealing with a very large data set, we will use the Minibatch K Means.

This operates on subsets of the data to compute the results more quickly and more accurately, just like the K-means algorithm, because I told you this data set is really huge. Even though this is a single image, the number of pixel combinations can come up to 16 million, which is a lot. Now each pixel is considered as a data point when you've taken image into consideration. When you have data points and data values, that's different.

When you're starting an image for image classification or image segmentation, each and every pixel is considered. So, basically, you're building matrices of all of these pixel values. So having 16 million pixels is a very huge data set. So, for that reason, we'll be using the Minibatch K Means. It's very similar to K-means. The only difference is that it'll operate on subsets of the data. Because the data set is too huge, it'll operate on subsets.

So, basically, we're making use of K-means in order to cluster these 16 million colour combinations into just 16 colours. So basically, we're gonna form 16 clusters in this data set. Now, the result is the recolouring of the original pixel where every pixel is assigned the colour of its closest cluster centre. Let's say that there are a couple of colours which are very close to green. So we're going to cluster all of these similar colours into one cluster.

We'll keep doing this until we get 16 clusters. So, obviously, to do this, we'll be using the clustering method, K-means. Let me show you what the output looks like. So, basically, this was the original image from the scikit data set, and this is the 16-color segmented image.

Basically, we have only 16 colours here. Here we can have around 16 million colours. Here there are only 16 colours. If you can't also, you can only see particular colours. Now obviously there's a lot of distortion over here, but this is how you study an image. Remove all the extra contrast that is there in an image.

You try to reduce the pixel to a smaller set of data as possible. The more varied pixels you have, the harder it is going to be for you to study the image for analysis. Now, obviously, there are some details which are lost in this. But overall, the image is still recognizable.

So here, basically, we've compressed this with a compression factor of around one million, because each cluster will have around one million data points in it, or pixel values in it, or pixels in it. Now this is an interesting application of K-means. There are actually better ways you can compress information on image.

So, basically, I showed you this example because I want you to understand the power of K-means algorithm. You can cluster a data set that is this huge into just 16 colours. Initially, there were 16 million, and now you can cluster it to 16 colours. So guys, K-means plays a very huge role in computer vision image processing, object detection, and so on.

It's a very important algorithm when it comes to detecting objects. So in self-driving cars and all can make use of such algorithms. So guys, that was all about unsupervised learning and supervised learning. Now it's the last type of machine learning,

REINFORCEMENT LEARNING

This is actually a very interesting part of machine learning, and it is quite difference from supervised and unsupervised. So, we'll be discussing all the concepts that are involved in reinforcement learning.

And also, reinforcement learning is a little more advanced. When I say advanced, I mean that it's been used in applications such as self-driving cars and is also a part of a lot of deep learning applications, such as AlphaGo and so on. So, reinforcement learning has a different concept to it itself.

So, we'll be discussing all the concepts under it. So just to brush up your information about reinforcement learning, reinforcement learning is a part of machine learning where an agent is put in an unknown environment, and he learns how to behave in this environment by performing certain actions and observing the rewards which it gets from these actions. Reinforcement learning is all about taking an appropriate action in order to maximize the reward in a particular situation.

DEMO (REINFORCEMENT LEARNING)

Now let's understand reinforcement learning with an analogy. Let's consider a scenario wherein a baby is learning how to walk. This scenario can go about in two different ways. The first is baby starts walking and it makes it to the candy.

REINFORCEMENT LEARNING ANALOGY

Scenario 1: Baby starts crawling and makes it to the candy

And since the candy is the end goal, the baby is very happy and it's positive. Meaning, the baby is happy and it received a positive reward. Now, the second way this can go in is that the baby starts walking, but it falls due to some hurdle between. That's really cute. So the baby gets hurt and it doesn't get to the candy.

It's negative because the baby is sad and it receives a negative reward. So just like how we humans learn from our mistakes by trial and error, reinforcement learning is also similar. Here we have an agent, and in this case, the agent is the baby, and the reward is the candy with many hurdles in between.

The agent is supposed to find the best possible path to

reach the reward. That is the main goal of reinforcement learning. Now the reinforcement learning process has two important components. It has something known as an agent and something known as an environment. Now the environment is the setting that the agent is acting on, and the agent represents the reinforcement learning algorithm.

The whole reinforcement learning is basically the agent. The environment is the setting in which you place the agent, and it is the setting wherein the agent takes various action. The reinforcement learning process starts when the environment sends a state to the agent. Now the agent, based on the observations it makes, it takes an action in response to that state.

Now, in turn, the environment will send the next state and the respective reward back to the agent. Now the agent will update its knowledge with the reward returned by the environment to evaluate its last actions. The loop continues until the environment sends a terminal state which means that the agent has accomplished all of its task.

COUNTER STRIKE EXAMPLE

1. The RL Agent (Player1) collects state S^0 from the environment

2. Based on the state S^0, the RL agent takes an action A^0, initially the action is random

3. The environment is now in a new state S^1

4. RL agent now gets a reward R^1 from the environment

5. The RL loop goes on until the RL agent is dead or reaches the destination

To understand this better, let's suppose that our agent is playing Counter Strike. The reinforcement learning process can be broken down into a couple of steps. The first step is the reinforcement learning agent, which is basically the player, he collects a state, S naught, from the environment.

So whenever you're playing Counter Strike, you start off with stage zero or stage one. You start off from the first level. Now based on this state, S naught, the reinforcement learning agent will take an action, A naught. So, guys, action can be anything that causes a result.

Now if the agent moves left or right in the game, that is also considered as an action. So initially, the action will be random, because the agent has no clue about the environment. Let's suppose that you're playing Counter Strike for the first time.

You have no idea about how to play it, so you'll just start randomly. You'll just go with whatever, whichever action you think is right. Now the environment is now in a stage one. After passing stage zero, the environment will go into stage one. Once the environment updates the stage to stage on, the reinforcement learning agent will get a reward R one from the environment.

This reward can be anything like additional points or you'll get additional weapons when you're playing Counter Strike. Now this reinforcement learning loop will go on until the agent is dead or reaches the destination, and it continuously outputs a sequence of state action and rewards. This exactly how reinforcement learning works. It starts with the agent being put in an environment, and the agent will randomly take some action in state zero.

After taking an action, depending on his action, he'll either get a reward and move on to state number one, or he will either die and go back to the same state. So this will keep happening until the agent reaches the last stage, or he dies or reaches his destination.

That's exactly how reinforcement learning works. Now reinforcement learning is the logic behind a lot of games these days. It's being implemented in various games, such as Dota. A lot of you who play Dota might know this. Now let's talk about a couple of reinforcement learning definitions or terminologies.

So, first, we have something known as the agent. Like I mentioned, an agent is the reinforcement learning algorithm that learns from trial and error. An agent is the one that takes actions like, for example, a solider in Counter Strike navigating through the game, going right, left, and all of that. Is the agent taking some action? The environment is because the world through which the agent moves.

Now the environment, basically, takes the agent's current state and action as input, and returns the agent's reward and its next state as the output. Next, we have something known as action. All the possible steps that an agent can take is considered as an action. Next, we have something known as state.

Now the current condition returned by the environment is known as a state. Reward is an instant return from the environment to apprise the last action of the reinforcement learning agent. All of these terms are pretty understandable.

Next, we have something known as policy. Now, policy is the approach that the agent uses to determine the next action based on the current state. Policy is basically the approach with which you go around in the environment.

we have something known as value. Now, the expected long-term return with a discount, as opposed to the short-term rewards R, is known as value. Now, terms like discount and value, I'll be discussing in the upcoming slides. Action-value is also very similar to the value, except it takes an extra parameter known as the current action.

Don't worry about action and Q value. We'll talk about all of this in the upcoming slides. So make yourself familiar with these terms, because we'll be seeing a whole lot of them this session. So, before we move any further, let's discuss a couple of more reinforcement learning concepts.

REWARD MAXIMIZATION

Reward maximization theory states that, *a RL agent must be trained in such a way that, he takes the best action so that the reward is maximum.*

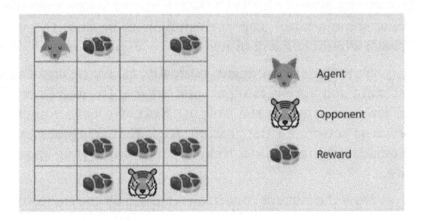

Now we have something known as the reward maximization. So if you haven't realized it already, the basic aim of reinforcement learning agent is to maximize the report. How does this happen? Let's try to understand this in a little more detail. So, basically the agent works based on the theory of reward maximization.

Now that's exactly why the agent must be trained in such a way that he takes the best action, so that the reward is maximal. Now let me explain a reward maximization with a small example. Now in this figure, you can see there is a fox, there is some meat, and there is a tiger.

Our reinforcement learning agent is the fox. His end goal is to eat the maximum amount of meat before being eaten by the tiger. Now because the fox is a very clever guy, he eats the meat that is closer to him, rather than the meat which is close to the tiger, because the closer he gets to the tiger, the higher are his chances of getting killed.

That's pretty obvious. Even if the reward near the tiger are bigger meat chunks, that'll be discounted. This is exactly what discount is. We just discussed it in the previous slide. This is done because of the uncertainty factor that the tiger might actually kill the fox.

Now the next thing to understand is how discounting of a reward works. Now, in order to understand discounting, we define a discount rate called gamma. The value of gamma is between zero and one. And the smaller the gamma, the larger the discount and so on. Now don't worry about these concepts, gamma and all of that.

We'll be seeing that in our practical demo today. So let's move on and discuss another concept known as exploration and exploitation trade-off. Now guys, before that, I hope all of you understood reward maximization. Basically, the main aim behind reinforcement learning is to maximize the rewards that an agent can get.

one of the most important concepts in reinforcement

learning is the exploration and exploitation trade-off. Now, exploration, like the name suggests, it's about exploring and capturing more information about an environment.

On the other hand, exploitation is about using the already known exploited information to heighten your reward. Now consider the same example that we saw previously. So here the fox eats only the meat chunks which are close to him.

He doesn't eat the bigger meat chunks which are at the top, even though the bigger meat chunks would get him more reward. So, if the fox only focuses on the closest reward, he will never reach the big chunks of meat. This process is known as exploitation. But if the fox decides to explore a bit, it can find the bigger reward, which is the big chunk of meat.

MARKOV'S DECISION PROCESS

The mathematical approach for mapping a solution in reinforcement learning is called *Markov Decision Process* (MDP)

The following parameters are used to attain a solution:

- Set of actions, A
- Set of states, S
- Reward, R
- Policy, π
- Value, V

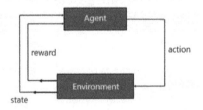

This is known as exploration. So this is the difference between exploitation and exploration. It's always best if the agent explores the environment, tries to figure out a way in which we can get the maximum number of rewards. Now let's discuss another important concept in reinforcement learning, which is known as the Markov's decision process. Basically, the mathematical approach for mapping a solution in reinforcement learning is called Markov's decision process.

It's the mathematics behind reinforcement learning.

Now, in a way, the purpose of reinforcement learning is to solve a Markov's decision process. Now in order to get a solution, there are a set of parameters in a Markov's decision process. There's a set of actions A, there's a set of states' S, a reward R, policy pi, and value V. Also, this image represents how a reinforcement learning works. There's an agent. The agent takes some action on the environment.

MARKOV'S DECISION PROCESS

Goal: Find the shortest path between A and D with minimum possible cost

In this problem,

- Set of states are denoted by nodes i.e. {A, B, C, D}
- Action is to traverse from one node to another {A -> B, C -> D}
- Reward is the cost represented by each edge
- Policy is the path taken to reach the destination {A -> B -> D}

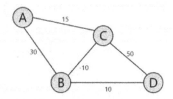

The environment, in turn, will reward the agent, and it will give him the next state. That's how reinforcement learning works so to sum everything up, what happens in Markov's decision process and reinforcement learning is the agent has to take an action A to transition from the start state to the end state S.

While doing so, the agent will receive some reward R for each action he takes. Now the series of action that are taken by the agent define the policy and the rewards collected to find the value. The main goal here is to maximize the rewards by choosing the optimum policy.

So you're gonna choose the best possible approach in order to maximize the rewards. That's the main aim of Markov's decision process. To understand Markov's decision process, let's look at a small example. I'm sure all of you already know about the shortest path problem.

We all had such problems and concepts in math to find

the shortest path. Now consider this representation over here, this figure. Here, our goal is to find the shortest path between two nodes. Let's say we're trying to find the shortest path between node A and node D.

Now each edge, as you can see, has a number linked with it. This number denotes the cost to traverse through that edge. So we need to choose a policy to travel from A to D in such a way that our cost is minimum. So in this problem, the set of states are denoted by the nodes A, B, C, D.

The action is to traverse from one node to the other. For example, if you're going from to A C, there is an action. C to B is an action. B to D is another action. The reward is the cost represented by each edge. Policy is the path taken to reach the destination.

So we need to make sure that we choose a policy in such a way that our cost is minimal. So what you can do is you can start off at node A, and you can take baby steps to reach your destination. Initially, only the next possible node is visible to you. So from A, you can either go to B or you can go to C. So if you follow the greedy approach and take the most optimum step, which is choosing A to C, instead of choosing A to B to C.

Now you're at node C and you want to traverse to node D. Again, you must choose your path very wisely. So if you traverse from A to C, and C to B, and B to D, your cost is the lest. But if you traverse from A to C to D, your cost will actually increase. Now you need to choose a policy that will minimize your cost over here.

So let's say, for example, the agent chose A to C to D. It came to node C, and then it directly chose D. Now the policy followed by our agent in this problem is exploitation type, because we didn't explore the other notes. We just selected three nodes and we traversed through them. And the policy we followed is not actually an optimal policy.

We must always explore more to find out the optimal

policy. Even if the other nodes are not giving us any more reward or is actually increasing our cost, we still have to explore and find out if those paths are actually better. That policy is actually better.

The method that we implemented here is known as the policy-based learning. Now the aim here is to find the best policy among all the possible policies. So guys, apart from policy-based, we also have value-based approach and action-based approach.

Value based emphasizes on maximizing the rewards. And in action base, we emphasize on each action taken by the agent. Now a point to note is that all of these learning approaches have a simple end goal.

The end goal is to effectively guide the agent through the environment, and acquire the greatest number of rewards. So this was very simple to understand Markov's decision process, exploitation and exploration trade-off, and we also discussed the different reinforcement learning definitions. I hope all of this was understandable.

Now let's move on and understand an algorithm known as Q-learning algorithm. So guys, Q-learning is one of the most important algorithms in reinforcement learning. And we'll discuss this algorithm with the help of a small example. We'll study this example, and then we'll implement the same example using Python, and we'll see how it works.

So this is how our demonstration looks for now. Now the problem statement is to place an agent in any one of the rooms numbered zero, one, two, three, and four. And the goal is for the agent to reach outside the building, which is room number five.

UNDERSTANDING Q-LEARNING

Place an agent in any one of the rooms (0,1,2,3,4) and the goal is to reach outside the building (room 5)

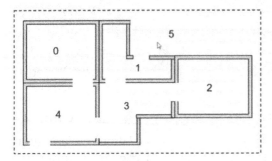

- 5 rooms in a building connected by doors
- each room is numbered 0 through 4
- The outside of the building can be thought of as one big room (5)
- Doors 1 and 4 lead into the building from room 5 (outside)

So, basically, this zero, one, two, three, four represents the building, and five represents a room which is outside the building. Now all these rooms are connected by those. Now these gaps that you see between the rooms are basically those, and each room is numbered from zero to four.

The outside of the building can be taught of as a big room which is room number five. Now if you've noticed this diagram, the door number one and door number four lead directly to room number five. From one, you can directly go to five, and from four, also, you can directly go to five.

But if you want to go to five from room number two, then you'll first have to go to room number three, room number one, and then room number five. So these are indirect links. Direct links are from room number one and room number four.

So I hope all of you are clear with the problem statement. You're basically going to have a reinforcement learning agent, and then agent has to traverse through all the rooms in such a way that he reaches room number five. To solve this problem, first, what we'll do is we'll represent the rooms on a graph.

UNDERSTANDING Q-LEARNING

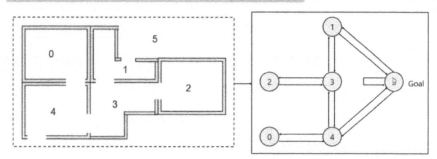

Let's represent the rooms on a graph, each room as a node, and each door as a link

Now each room is denoted as anode, and the links that are connecting these nodes are the doors. Alright, so we have node one to five, and the links between each of these nodes represent the doors. So, for example, if you look at this graph over here, you can see that there is a direct connection from one to five, meaning that you can directly go from room number one to your goal, which is room number five.

So, if you want to go from room number three to five, you can either go to room number one, and then go to five, or you can go from room number three to four, and then to five. So guys, remember, end goal is to reach room number five. Now to set the room number five as the goal state, what we'll do is we'll associate a reward value to each door.

The doors that lead immediately to the goal will have an instant reward of 100. So, basically, one to five will have a reward of hundred, and four to five will also have a reward of hundred. Now other doors that are not directly connected to the target room will have a zero reward, because they do not directly lead us to that goal. So let's say you placed the agent in room number three. So to go from room number three to one, the agent will get a reward of zero. And to go from one to five, the agent will get a reward of hundred. Now because the doors are two-way, the two arrows are assigned to each

UNDERSTANDING Q-LEARNING

Next step is to associate a reward value to each door:

- doors that lead directly to the goal have a reward of 100

- Doors not directly connected to the target room have zero reward

- Because doors are two-way, two arrows are assigned to each room

- Each arrow contains an instant reward value

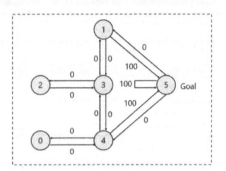

You can see an arrow going towards the room and one coming from the room. So each arrow contains an instant reward as shown in this figure. Now of course room number five will loop back to itself with a reward of hundred, and all other direct connections to the goal room will carry a reward of hundred. Now in Q-learning, the goal is to reach the state with the highest reward. So that if the agent arrives at the goal, it will remain there forever.

So I hope all of you are clear with this diagram. Now, the terminologies in Q-learning include two terms, state and action. Okay, your room basically represents the state. So if you're in state two, it basically means that you're in room number two. Now the action is basically the moment of the agent from one room to the other room. Let's say you're going from room number two to room number three. That is basically an action. Now let's consider some more example.

Let's say you place the agent in room number two and he has to get to the goal. So your initial state will be state number two or room number two. Then from room number two, you'll go to room number three, which is state three. Then from state three, you can either go back to state two or go to state one or state four. If you go to state four, from there you can directly go to your goal room, which is five.

This is how the agent is going to traverse. Now in order to depict the rewards that you're going to get, we're going to create a matrix known as the reward matrix. Okay, this is represented by R or also known as the R matrix. Now the minus one in this table represents null values. That is basically where there isn't a link between the nodes that is represented as minus one. Now there is no link between zero and zero.

That's why it's minus one. Now if you look at this diagram, there is no direct link from zero to one. That's why I've put minus one over here as well. But if you look at zero comma four, we have a value of zero over here, which means that you can traverse from zero to four, but your reward is going to be zero, because four is not your goal state.

However, if you look at the matrix, look at one comma five. In one comma five, we have a reward value of hundred. This is because you can directly go from room number one to five, and five is the end goal. That's why we've assigned a reward of hundred. Similarly, for four comma five, we have a reward of hundred. And for five comma five, we have a reward of hundred. Zeroes basically represent other links, but they are zero because they do not lead to the end goal.

UNDERSTANDING Q-LEARNING

Next step is to associate a reward value to each door:

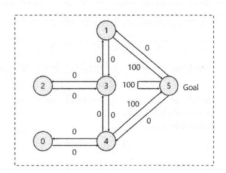

- doors that lead directly to the goal have a reward of 100

- Doors not directly connected to the target room have zero reward

- Because doors are two-way, two arrows are assigned to each room

- Each arrow contains an instant reward value

So I hope you all understood the reward matrix. It's very simple. Now before we move any further, we'll be creating another matrix known as the equitable Q matrix. Now the Q matrix basically represents the memory of what the agent has learned through experience. The rules of the Q matrix will represent the current state of the agent.

The columns will represent the next possible actions leading to the next state, and the formula to calculate the Q matrix is this formula, right? Here we have Q state comma action, R state comma action, which is nothing but the reward matrix. Then we have a parameter known as the Gamma parameter, which I'll explain shortly. And then we are multiplying this with a maximum of Q next state comma all actions.

Now don't worry if you haven't understood this formula. I'll explain this with a small example. For now, let's understand what a Gamma parameter is. So, basically, the value of Gamma will be between zero and one. If Gamma is closer to zero, it means that the agent will tend to consider only immediate rewards. Now, if the Gamma is closer to one, it means that the agent will consider future rewards with greater weight.

UNDERSTANDING Q-LEARNING

The terminology in Q-Learning includes the terms state and action:
• Room (including room 5) represents a state
• agent's movement from one room to another represents an action
• In the figure, a state is depicted as a node, while "action" is represented by the arrows

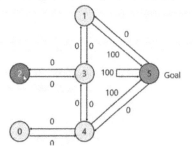

Example (Agent traverse from room 2 to room5):

1. Initial state = state 2

2. State 2 -> state 3

3. State 3 -> state (2, 1, 4)

4. State 4 -> state 5

Now what exactly I'm trying to say is if Gamma is closer to one, then we'll be performing something known as exploitation. I hope you all remember what exploitation and exploration trade-off is. So, if your gamma is closer to zero, it means that the agent is not going to explore the environment. Instead, it'll just choose a couple of states, and it'll just traverse through those states. But if your gamma parameter is closer to one, it means that the agent will traverse through all possible states, meaning that it'll perform exploration, not exploitation.

So the closer your gamma parameter is to one, the more your agent will explore. This is exactly what Gamma parameter is. If you want to get the best policy, it's always practical that you choose a Gamma parameter which is closer to one. We want the agent to explore the environment as much as possible so that it can get the best policy and the maximum rewards.

I hope this is clear. Now let me just tell you what a Q-learning algorithm is step by step. So you begin the Q-learning algorithm by setting the Gamma parameter and the environment rewards in matrix R. Okay, so, first, you'll have set these two values.

UNDERSTANDING Q-LEARNING

We can put the state diagram and the instant reward values into a reward table, matrix R.

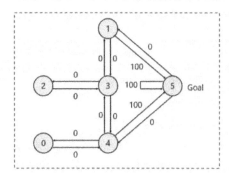

	Action					
State	0	1	2	3	4	5
0	-1	-1	-1	-1	0	-1
1	-1	-1	-1	0	-1	100
2	-1	-1	-1	0	-1	-1
3	-1	0	0	-1	0	-1
4	0	-1	-1	0	-1	100
5	-1	0	-1	-1	0	100

$R =$

The -1's in the table represent null values

We've already calculated the reward matrix. We need to set the Gamma parameter. Next, you'll initialize the matrix Q to zero. Now why do you do this? Now, if you remember, I said that Q matrix is basically the memory of the agent. Initially, obviously, the agent has no memory of the environment. It's new to the environment and you're placing it randomly anywhere.

So, it has zero memory. That's why you initialize the matrix Q to zero. After that, you'll select a random initial state, and you place your agent in that initial state. Then you'll set this initial state as your current state.

Now from the current state, you'll select some action that will lead you to the next state. Then you'll basically get the maximum Q value for this next state, based on all the possible actions that we take. Then you'll keep computing the skew value until you reach the goals state. Now that might be a little bit confusing, so let's look at this entire thing with a small example. Let's say that first, you're gonna begin with setting your Gamma parameter. So I'm setting my Gamma parameter to 0.8 which is pretty close to one.

UNDERSTANDING Q-LEARNING

Add another matrix Q representing the memory of what the agent has learned through experience.
- The rows of matrix Q represent the current state of the agent
- columns represent the possible actions leading to the next state
- Formula to calculate the Q matrix:

Q(state, action) = R(state, action) + Gartyma * Max [Q(next state, all actions)]

Note

The Gamma parameter has a range of 0 to 1 (0 <= Gamma > 1).
- If Gamma is closer to zero, the agent will tend to consider only immediate rewards.
- If Gamma is closer to one, the agent will consider future rewards with greater weight

This means that our agent will explore the environment as much as possible. And also, I'm setting the initial state as room one. Meaning, I'm in state one or I'm in room one. So basically, your agent is going to be in room number one. The next step is to initialize the Q matrix as zero matrix.

So, this is a Q matrix. You can see that everything is set

to zero, because the agent has no memory at all. He hasn't traversed to any node, so he has no memory. Now since the agent is in room one, he can either go to room number three or he can go to room number five.

Let's randomly select room number five. So, from room number five, you're going to calculate the maximum Q value for the next state based on all possible actions.

So, all the possible actions from room number five is one, four, and five. So, basically, the traversing from Q one comma five, that's why I put one comma five over here, state comma action. Your reward matrix will have R one comma five. Now R one comma five is basically hundred. That's why I put hundred over here. Now your comma parameter is 0.8. So, guys, what I'm doing here is I'm just substituting the values in this formula.

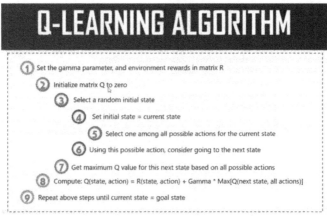

So, let me just repeat this whole thing. Q state comma action. So, you're in state number one, correct? And your action is you're going to room number five. So, your Q state comma action is one comma five. Again, your reward matrix R one comma five is hundred.

So, here's you're gonna put hundred, plus your Gamma parameter. Your Gamma parameter is 0.8. Then you're going to calculate the maximum Q value for the next state based on all possible actions. So, let's look at the next state. From room number five, you can go to either one. You can go to four or you can go to five.

So, your actions are five comma one, five comma four, and five comma five. That's exactly what I mentioned over here. Q five comma one, Q five comma four, and Q five comma five. You're basically putting all the next possible actions from state number five. From here, you'll calculate the maximum Q value that you're getting for each of these.

Now your Q value is zero, because, initially, your Q matrix is set to zero. So, you're going to get zero for Q five comma one, five comma four, and five comma five. So that's why you'll get 0.8 and zero, and hence your Q one comma five becomes hundred. This hundred comes from R one comma five. I hope all of you understood this. So next, what you'll do is you'll update this one comma five value in your Q matrix, because you just calculated Q one comma five.

Q-LEARNING EXAMPLE

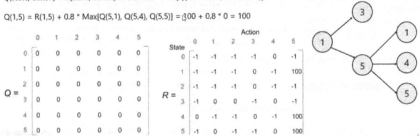

First step is to set the value of the learning parameter Gamma = 0.8, and the initial state as Room 1.

Next, initialize matrix Q as a zero matrix:
• From room 1 you can either go to room 3 or 5, let's select room 5.
• From room 5, calculate maximum Q value for this next state based on all possible actions:
Q(state, action) = R(state, action) + Gamma * Max[Q(next state, all actions)]

Q(1,5) = R(1,5) + 0.8 * Max[Q(5,1), Q(5,4), Q(5,5)] = 100 + 0.8 * 0 = 100

$$Q = \begin{bmatrix} & 0 & 1 & 2 & 3 & 4 & 5 \\ 0 & 0 & 0 & 0 & 0 & 0 & 0 \\ 1 & 0 & 0 & 0 & 0 & 0 & 0 \\ 2 & 0 & 0 & 0 & 0 & 0 & 0 \\ 3 & 0 & 0 & 0 & 0 & 0 & 0 \\ 4 & 0 & 0 & 0 & 0 & 0 & 0 \\ 5 & 0 & 0 & 0 & 0 & 0 & 0 \end{bmatrix}$$

State	Action 0	1	2	3	4	5
0	-1	-1	-1	-1	0	-1
1	-1	-1	-1	0	-1	100
2	-1	-1	-1	0	-1	-1
3	-1	0	0	-1	0	-1
4	0	-1	-1	0	-1	100
5	-1	0	-1	-1	0	100

R =

So, I've updated it over here. Now for the next episode, we'll start with a randomly chosen initial state. Again, let's say that we randomly chose state number three. Now from room number three, you can either go to room number one, two or four.

Let's randomly select room number one. Now, from room number five, you'll calculate the maximum Q value for the next possible actions. So let's calculate the Q formula for this. So your Q state comma action becomes three comma one, because you're in state number three and your action is you're going to room number one.

So your R three comma one, let's see what R three comma one is. R three comma one is zero. So you're going to put zero over here, plus your Gamma parameter, which is 0.8, and then you're going to check the next possible actions from room number one, and you're going to choose the maximum value from these two.

So Q one comma three and Q one comma five denote your next possible actions from room number one. So Q one comma three is zero, but Q one comma five is hundred. So we just calculated this hundred in the previous step. So, out of zero and hundred, hundred is your maximum value, so you're going to choose hundred. Now 0.8 into hundred is nothing but 80.

So again, your Q matrix gets updated. You see an 80 over here. So, basically what you're doing is as you're taking actions, you're updating your Q value, you're just calculating the Q value at every step, you're putting it in your Q matrix so that your agent remembers that, okay, when I went from room number one to room number five, I had a Q value of hundred.

Similarly, three to one gave me a Q value of 80. So basically, this Q matrix represents the memory of your agent. I hope all of you are clear with this. So basically, what we're gonna do is we're gonna keep iterating through this loop until we've gone through all possible states and reach the goal state, which is five.

Also, our main aim here is to find the most optimum policy to get to room number five. Now let's implement the exact same thing using Python. So that was a lot of theory. Now let's understand how this is done practically.

DEMO (REINFORCEMENT LEARNING)

Alright, so we begin by importing your library. We're gonna be using the NumPy library over here. After that, we'll import the R matrix. We've already created the R matrix. This is the exact matrix that I showed you a couple of minutes ago.

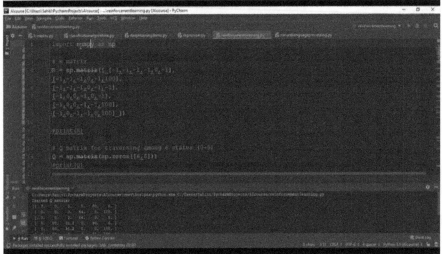

So I've created a matrix called R and I've basically stored all the rewards in it. If you want to see the R matrix, let me print it. So, basically, this is your R matrix. If you remember, node one to five, you have a reward of hundred.

Node four to five, you have a reward of hundred, and five to five, you have a reward of hundred, because all of these nodes directly lead us to the reward. Correct? Next, what we're doing is we're creating a Q matrix which is basically a six into six matrixes.

Which represents all the states, zero to five. And this matrix is basically zero. After, that we're setting the Gamma parameter. Now guys, you can play around with this code, and you know you can change the comma parameter to 0.7 or 0.9 and see how much more the agent will explore or whether you perform exploitation.

Here I've set the Gamma parameter 0.8 which is a pretty good number. Now what I'm doing is I'm setting the initial state as one. You can randomly choose this state according to your needs. I've set the initial state as one.

Now, this function will basically give me all the available actions from my initial state. Since I've set my initial state as one, it'll give me all the possible actions. Here what I'm doing is since my initial state is one, I'm checking in my row number one, which value is equal to zero or greater than zero. Those denote my available actions.

Q-LEARNING EXAMPLE

First step is to set the value of the learning parameter Gamma = 0.8, and the initial state as Room 1.

Next, initialize matrix Q as a zero matrix:
- From room 1 you can either go to room 3 or 5, let's select room 5.
- From room 5, calculate maximum Q value for this next state based on all possible actions:

Q(state, action) = R(state, action) + Gamma * Max[Q(next state, all actions)]

Q(1,5) = R(1,5) + 0.8 * Max[Q(5,1), Q(5,4), Q(5,5)] = 100 + 0.8 * 0 = 100

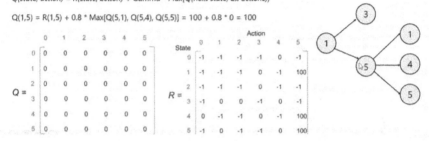

So, look at our row number one. Here we have one zero and we have a hundred over here. This is one comma four and this is one comma five. So if you look at the row number one, since I've selected the initial state as one, we'll consider row number one. Okay, what I'm doing is in row number one, I have two numbers which are either equal to zero or greater than zero.

These denote my possible actions. One comma three has the value of zero and one comma five has the value of hundred, which means that the agent can either go to room number three or it can go to room number five. What I'm trying to say is from room number one, you can basically go to room number three or room number five.

This is exactly what I've coded over here. If you remember the reward matrix, from one you can traverse to only room number three directly and room number five directly. Okay, that's exactly what I've mentioned in my code over here.

So, this will basically give me the available actions from my current state. Now once I've moved to me next state, I need to check the available actions from that state. What I'm doing over here is basically this. If you're remember, from room number one, we can go to three and five, correct? And from three and five, I'll randomly select the state.

And from that state, I need to find out all possible actions. That's exactly what I've done over here. Okay. Now this will randomly choose an action for me from all my available actions. Next, we need to update our Q matrix, depending on the actions that we took, if you remember.

So that's exactly what this update function is four. Now guys, this entire is for calculating the Q value. I hope all of you remember the formula, which is Q state comma action, R state comma action plus Gamma into max value. Max value will basically give me the maximum value out of the all possible actions. I'm basically computing this formula.

Now this will just update the Q matrix. Coming to the training phase, what we're gonna do is we are going to set a range. Here I've set a range of 10,000, meaning that my agent will perform 10,000 iterations. You can set this depending on your own needs, and 10,000 iteration is a pretty huge number.

So, basically, my agent is going to go through 10,000 possible iterations in order to find the best policy. Now this is the exact same thing that we did earlier. We're setting the current state, and then we're choosing the available action from the current state. The from there, we'll choose an action at random.

Here we'll calculate a Q value and we'll update the Q value in the matrix. Alright. And here I'm doing nothing, but I'm printing the trained Q matrix. This was the training phase. Now the testing phase, basically, you're going to randomly choose a current state. You're gonna choose a current state, and you're going to keep looping through this entire code, until you reach the goal state, which is room number five.

That's exactly what I'm doing in this whole thing. Also, in the end, I'm printing the selected part. That is basically the policy that the agent took to reach room number five. Now if I set the current state as one, it should give me the best policy to reach to room number five from room number one. Alright, let's run this code, and let's see if it's giving us that.

Now before that happens, I want you to check and tell me which is the best possible way to get from room number one to room number five. It's obviously directly like this. One to five is the best policy to get from room number one to room number five.

So we should get an output of one comma five. That's exactly what we're getting this is a Q matrix with all the Q values, and here we are getting the selected path. So if your current state is one, your best policy is to go from one to five.

Now, if you want to change your current state, let's say we set the current state to two. And before we run the code, let's see which is the best possible way to get to room number five from room number two. From room number two, you can go to three, then you can go to one, and then you can go to five.

UNDERSTANDING Q-LEARNING

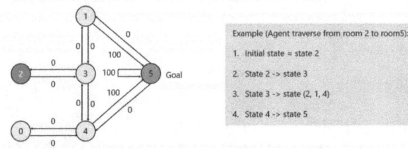

The terminology in Q-Learning includes the terms state and action:
• Room (including room 5) represents a state
• agent's movement from one room to another represents an action
• In the figure, a state is depicted as a node, while "action" is represented by the arrows

Example (Agent traverse from room 2 to room5):

1. Initial state = state 2

2. State 2 -> state 3

3. State 3 -> state (2, 1, 4)

4. State 4 -> state 5

This will give you a reward of hundred, or you can go to room number three, then go to four, and then go to five. This will also give you a reward of hundred. Our path should be something like that. Let's save it and let's run the file.

So, basically, from stage two, you're going to say three, then to four, and then to five. This is our best possible path from two to room number five. So, guys, this is exactly how the Q learning algorithm works, and this was a simple implementation of the entire example that I just told you. Now if any of you still have doubts regarding Q learning or reinforcement learning,

No, we're done with machine learning. We've completed the whole machine learning model. We've understood reinforcement learning, supervised learning, unsupervised learning, and so on. Before I'll get to deep learning, a very common misconception.

AI VS MACHINE LEARNING
VS DEEP LEARNING

A lot of people get confused between AI machine learning and deep learning, because, you know, artificial intelligence, machine learning and deep learning are very common applications. For example, Siri is an application of artificial intelligence, machine learning, and deep learning.

So how are these three connected? Are they the same thing or how exactly is the relationship between artificial intelligence, machine learning, and deep learning? This is what I'll be discussing.

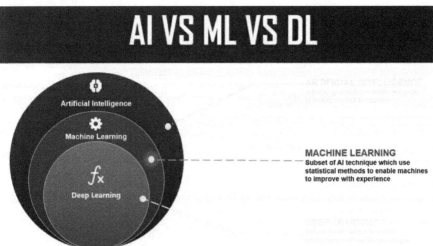

now artificial intelligence is basically the science of getting machines to mimic the behaviour of human beings. But when it comes to machine learning, machine learning is a subset of artificial intelligence that focuses on getting machines to make decisions by feeding them data. That's exactly what machine learning is.

It is a subset of artificial intelligence. Deep learning, on the other hand, is a subset of machine learning that uses the concept of neural networks to solve complex problems. So, to sum it up, artificial intelligence, machine learning, and deep learning, are interconnected fields.

Machine learning and deep learning aids artificial intelligence by providing a set of algorithms and neural networks to solve data-driven problems. That's how AI, machine learning, and deep learning are related. I hope all of you have cleared your misconceptions and doubts about AI, ML, and deep learning.

LIMITATIONS OF MACHINE LEARNING

The first limitation is machine learning is not capable enough to handle high dimensional data. This is where the input and the output is very large. So handling and processing such type of data becomes very complex and it takes up a lot of resources.

LIMITATIONS OF ML

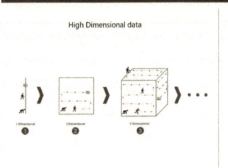

High Dimensional data

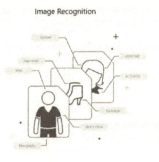

Image Recognition

This is also sometimes known as the curse of dimensionality. So, to understand this in simpler terms, look at the image shown on this slide. Consider a line of hundred yards and let's say that you dropped a coin somewhere on the line.

Now it's quite convenient for you to find the coin by simply walking along the line. This is very simple because this line is considered as single dimensional entity. Now next, you consider that you have a square of hundred yards, and let's say you dropped a coin somewhere in between.

Now it's quite evident that you're going to take more time to find the coin within that square as compared to the previous scenario. The square is, let's say, a two-dimensional entity. Let's take it a step ahead and let's consider a cube. Okay, let's say there's a cube of 500 yards and you have dropped a coin somewhere in between this cube.

Now it becomes even more difficult for you to find the coin this time, because this is a three-dimensional entity. So, as your dimension increases, the problem becomes more complex. So if you observe that the complexity is increasing the increase in your dimensions, and in real life, the high dimensional data that we're talking about has thousands of dimensions that makes it very complex to handle and process. and a high dimensional data can easily be found in used cases like image processing, natural language processing, image translation, and so on.

Now in K-means itself, we saw that we had 16 million possible colours. That is a lot of data. So, this is why machine learning is restricted. It cannot be used in the process of image recognition because image recognition and images have a lot of pixels and they have a lot of high dimensional data.

That's why machine learning becomes very restrictive when it comes to such use's cases. Now the second major challenge is to tell the computer what are the features it should look for that will play an important role in predicted the outcome and in getting a good accuracy. Now this process is something known as feature extraction.

LIMITATIONS OF ML

One of the big challenges with traditional Machine Learning models is a process called feature extraction. For complex problems such as object recognition or handwriting recognition, this is a huge challenge.

Now feeding raw data to the algorithm rarely works, and this is the reason why feature extraction is a critical part of machine learning workflow. Now the challenge for the programmer here increases because the effectiveness of the algorithm depends on how insightful the programmer is. As a programmer, you have to tell the machine that these are the features.

And depending on these features, you have to predict the outcome. That's how machine learning works. So far, in all our demos, we saw that we were providing predictor variables. we were providing input variables that will help us predict the outcome.

We were trying to find correlations between variables, and we're trying to find out the variable that is very important in predicting the output variable. So, this becomes a challenge for the programmer.

That's why it's very difficult to apply machine learning model to complex problems like object recognition, handwriting recognition, natural language processing, and so on. Now all these problems and all these limitations in machine learning led to the introduction of deep learning.

INTRODUCTION TO DEEP LEARNING

Now we're gonna discuss about deep learning. Now deep learning is one of the only methods by which we can overcome the challenges of feature extraction. This is because deep learning models are capable of learning to focus on the right features by themselves, which requires very little guidance from the programmer.

WHY DEEP LEARNING?

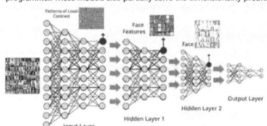

Deep Learning models are capable to focus on the right features by themselves, requiring little guidance from the programmer. These models also partially solve the dimensionality problem.

The idea behind Deep Learning is to build learning algorithms that mimic brain.

Basically, deep learning mimics the way our brain functions. That is it learns from experience. So in deep learning, what happens is feature extraction happens automatically. You need very little guidance by the programmer.

So deep learning will learn the model, and it will understand which feature or which variable is important in predicting the outcome. Let's say you have millions of predictor variables for a particular problem statement. How are you going to sit down and understand the significance of each of these predictor variables it's going to be almost impossible to sit down with so many features.

That's why we have deep learning. Whenever there's high dimensionality data or whenever the data is really large and it has a lot of features and a lot of predictor variables, we use deep learning. Deep learning will extract features on its own and understand which features are important in predicting your output. So that's the main idea behind deep learning.

Let me give you a small example also. Suppose we want to make a system that can recognize the face of different people in an image. Okay, so, basically, we're creating a system that can identify the faces of different people in in image. If we solve this by using the typical machine learning algorithms, we'll have to define facial features like eyes, nose, ears, et cetera.

Okay, and then the system will identify which features are more important for which person. Now, if you consider deep learning for the same example, deep learning will automatically find out the features which are important for classification, because it uses the concept of neural networks, whereas in machine learning we have to manually define these features on our own. That's the main difference between deep learning and machine learning. Now the next question is how does deep learning work?

HOW DEEP LEARNING WORKS?

HOW DEEP LEARNING WORK?

Deep learning is a form of machine learning that uses a model of computing that's very much inspired by the structure of the brain, so lets understand that first.

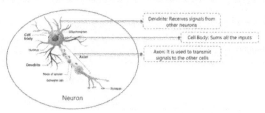

Biological Neuron

when people started coming up with deep learning, their main aim was to re-engineer the human brain. Okay, deep learning studies the basic unit of a brain called the brain cell or a neuron. All of your biology students will know what I'm talking about.

So, basically, deep learning is inspired from our brain structure. Okay, in our brains, we have something known as neurons, and these neurons are replicated in deep learning as artificial neurons, which are also called perceptron's. Now, before we understand how artificial neural networks or artificial neurons work, let's understand how these biological neurons work, because I'm not sure how many of you are bio students over here.

So let's understand the functionality of biological neurons and how we can mimic this functionality in a perceptron or in an artificial neuron. So, guys, if you loo at this image, this is basically an image of a biological neuron. If you focus on the structure of the biological neuron, it has something known dendrites. These dendrites are basically used to receive inputs.

Now the inputs are basically found in the cell body, and it's passed on the next biological neuron. So, through dendrites, you're going to receive signals from other neurons, basically, input. Then the cell body will sum up all these inputs, and the axon will transmit this input to other neurons.

The axon will fire up through some threshold, and it will get passed onto the next neuron. So similar to this, a perceptron or an artificial neuron receives multiple inputs, and applies various transformations and functions and provides us an output. These multiple inputs are nothing but your input variables or your predictor variables.

You're feeding input data to an artificial neuron or to a perceptron, and this perceptron will apply various functions and transformations, and it will give you an output. Now just like our brain consists of multiple connected neurons called neural networks, we also build something known as a network of artificial neurons called artificial neural networks. So that's the basic concept behind deep learning. To sum it up, what exactly is deep learning?

WHAT IS DEEP LEARNING?

Now deep learning is a collection of statistical machine learning techniques used to learn feature hierarchies based on the concept of artificial neural networks. So the main idea behind deep learning is artificial neural networks which work exactly like how our brain works.

Now in this diagram, you can see that there are a couple of layers. The first layer is known as the input layer. This is where you'll receive all the inputs. The last layer is known as the output layer which provides your desired output. Now, all the layers which are there between your input layer and your output layer are known as the hidden layers.

Now, they can be any number of hidden layers, thanks to all the resources that we have these days. So you can have hundreds of hidden layers in between. Now, the number of hidden layers and the number of perceptron's in each of these layers will entirely depend on the problem or on the use case that you're trying to solve. So this is basically how deep learning works. So let's look at the example that we saw earlier.

DEEP LEARNING USE CASE

Here what we want to do is we want to perform image recognition using deep networks. First, what we're gonna do is we are going to pass this high dimensional data to the input layer.

To match the dimensionality of the input data, the input layer will contain multiple sub layers of perceptron's so that it consumes the entire input. Okay, so you'll have multiple sub layers of perceptron's.

UNDERSTANDING DEEP LEARNING

Image recognition using Deep Networks:

1. Pass the high dimensional data to the input layer

2. Output received from the input layer contains patterns which are extracted

3. Output will be fed to the Hidden layer 1

4. Hidden layer 2 will be able to form the entire faces

5. The output layer performs classification

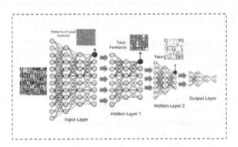

Now, the output received from the input layer will contain patterns and will only be able to identify the edges of the images, based on the contrast levels. This output will then be fed to hidden layer number one where it'll be able to identify facial features like your eyes, nose, ears, and all of that. Now from here, the output will be fed to hidden layer number two, where it will be able to form entire faces it'll go deeper into face recognition, and this output of the hidden layer will be sent to the output layer or any other hidden layer that is there before the output layer.

Now, finally, the output layer will perform classification,

based on the result that you'd get from your previous layers. So, this is exactly how deep learning works. This is a small analogy that I use to make you understand what deep learning is. Now let's understand what a single layer perceptron is. So like I said, perceptron is basically an artificial neuron.

SINGLE LAYER PERCEPTRON

For something known as single layer and multiple layer perceptron, we'll first focus on single layer perceptron. Now before I explain what a perceptron really is, you should know that perceptron's are linear classifiers. A single layer perceptron is a linear or a binary classifier.

A PERCEPTRON

An Artificial Neuron or a Perceptron is a linear model used for binary classification. It models a neuron which has a set of inputs, each of which is given a specific weight. The neuron computes some function on these weighted inputs and gives the output.

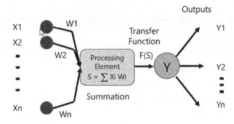

Artificial Neural Network

Perceptron or Artificial Neuron

It is used mainly in supervised learning, and it helps to classify the given input data into separate classes. So, this diagram basically represents a perceptron. A perceptron has multiple inputs. It has a set of inputs labelled X one, X two, until X n.

Now each of these inputs is given a specific weight. Okay, so W one represents the weight of input X one. W two represents the weight of input X two, and so on. Now how you assign these weights is a different thing altogether.

But for now, you need to know that each input is assigned a particular weightage. Now what a perceptron does is it computes some functions on these weighted inputs, and it will give you the output. So, basically, these weighted inputs go through something known as summation.

Okay, summation is nothing but the product of each of your input with its respective weight. Now after the summation is done, this passed onto transfer function. A transfer function is nothing but an activation function. I'll be discussing more about this in a minute. The activation function. And from the activation function, you'll get the outputs Y one, Y two, and so on.

So guys, you need to understand four important parts in a perceptron. So, firstly, you have the input values. You have X one, X two, X three. You have something known as weights and bias, and then you have something known as the net sum and finally the activation function.

Now, all the inputs X are multiplied with the respective weights. So, X one will be multiplied with W one. This is known as the summation. After this, you'll add all the multiplied values, and we'll call them as the weighted sum. This is done using the summation function.

Now we'll apply the weighted sum to a correct activation function. Now, a lot of people have a confusion about activation function. Activation function is also known as the transfer function. Now, in order to understand activation function, this word stems from the way neurons in a human brain work. The neuron becomes activate only after a certain potential is reached.

That threshold is known as the activation protection. Therefore, mathematically, it can be represented by a function that reaches saturation after a threshold. Okay, we have a lot of activation functions like signum, sigmoid, tan, hedge, and so on. You can think of activation function as a function that maps the input to the respective output.

And now I also spoke about weights and bias. Now why do we assign weights to each of these inputs? What weights do is they show a strength of a particular input, or how important a particular input is for predicting the final output. So, basically, the weightage of an input denotes the importance of that input.

Now, our bias basically allows us to shift the activation function in order to get a precise output. So that was all about perceptron's. Now in order to make you understand perceptron's better, let's look at a small analogy. Suppose that you wanna go to a party happening near your hose. Now your decision will depend on a set of factors.

First is how is the weather. Second probably is your wife, or your girlfriend, or your boyfriend going with you. And third, is there any public transport available? Let's say these are the three factors that you're going to consider before you go to a party.

So, depending on these predictor variables or these features, you're going to decide whether you're going to stay at home or go and party. Now, how is the weather is going to be your first input. We'll represent this with a value X one. Is your wife going with you is another input X two.

Any public transport is available is another input X three. Now, X one will have two values, one and zero. One represents that the weather is good. Zero represents weather is bad. Similarly, one represents that your wife is going, and zero represents that your wife is not going.

And in X three, again, one represents that there is public transport, and zero represents that there is no public transport. Now your output will either be one or zero. One means you are going to the party, and zero means you will be sitting at home.

Now in order to understand weightage, let's say that the most important factor for you is your weather. If the weather is good, it means that you will 100% go to the party. Now if you weather is not good; you've decided that you'll sit at home.

So the maximum weightage is for your weather variable. So if your weather is really good, you will go to the party. It is a very important factor in order to understand whether you're going to sit at home or you're going to go to the party. So, basically, if X one equal to one, your output will be one. Meaning that if your weather is good, you'll go to the party.

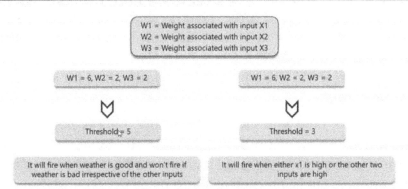

PERCEPTRON LEARNING ANALOGY

W1 = Weight associated with input X1
W2 = Weight associated with input X2
W3 = Weight associated with input X3

W1 = 6, W2 = 2, W3 = 2   W1 = 6, W2 = 2, W3 = 2

Threshold = 5   Threshold = 3

It will fire when weather is good and won't fire if weather is bad irrespective of the other inputs   It will fire when either x1 is high or the other two inputs are high

Now let's randomly assign weights to each of our input. W one is the weight associated with input X one. W two is the weight with X two and W three is the weight associated with X three. Let's say that your W one is six, your W two is two, and W three is two.

Now by using the activation function, you're going to set a threshold of five. Now this means that it will fire when the weather is good and won't fire if the weather is bad, irrespective of the other inputs.

Now here, because your weightage is six, so, basically, if you consider your first input which has a weightage of six, that means you're 100% going to go. Let's say you're considering only the second input.

This means that you're not going to go, because your weightage is two and your threshold is five. So if your weightage is below your threshold, it means that you're not going to go. Now let's consider another scenario where our threshold is three.

This means that it'll fire when either X one is high or the other two inputs are high. Now W two is associated with your wife is going or not. Let's say the weather is bad and you have no public transportation, meaning that your x one and x three is zero, and only your x two is one.

Now if your x two is one, your weightage is going to be two. If your weightage is two, you will not go because the threshold value is set to three. The threshold value is set in such a way that if X two and X three are combined together, only then you'll go, or only if x one is true, then you'll go. So you're assigning threshold in such a way that you will go for sure if the weather is good.

This is how you assign threshold. This is nothing but your activation function. So guys, I hope all of you understood, the most amount of weightage is associated with the input that is very important in predicting your output.

This is exactly how a perceptron works. Now let's look at the limitations of a perceptron. Now in a perceptron, there are no hidden layers. There's only an input layer, and there is an output layer. We have no hidden layers in between. And because of this, you cannot classify non-linearly separable data points.

Okay, if you have data, like in this figure, how will you separate this. You cannot use a perceptron to do this. Alright, so complex problems that involve a lot of parameters cannot be solved by a single layer perceptron. That's why we need something known as multiple layer perceptron. So now we'll discuss something known as multilayer perceptron.

MULTI-LAYER PERCEPTRON (ANN)

A multilayer perceptron has the same structure of a single layer perceptron, but with one or more hidden layer. Okay, and that's why it's consider as a deep neural network. So in a single layer perceptron, we had only input layer, output layer.

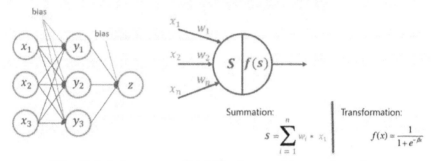

A Multi-layer Perceptron has the same structure of a single layer perceptron but with one or more hidden layers and is thus considered a deep neural network.

We didn't have any hidden layer. Now when it comes to multi-layer perceptron, there are hidden layers in between, and then there is the output layer. It was in this similar manner, like I said, first, you'll have the input X one, X two, X three, and so on. And each of these inputs will be assigned some weight. W one, W two, W three, and so on.

Then you'll calculate the weighted summation of each of these inputs and their weights. After that, you'll send them to the transformation or the activation function, and you'll finally get the output. Now, the only thing is that you'll have multiple hidden layers in between, one or more than one hidden layers.

MULTILAYER PERCEPTRON

- The weights between the units are the primary means of long-term information storage in neural networks

- Updating the weights is the primary way the neural network learns new information

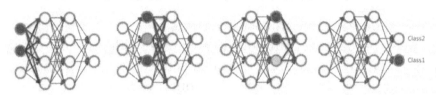

A set of inputs are passed to the first hidden layer, the activations from that layer are passed to the next layer and so on, until you reach the output layer.

So, guys, this is how a multilayer perceptron works. It works on the concept of feed forward neural networks. Feed forward means every node at each level or each layer is connected to every other node. So that's what feed forward networks are. Now when it comes to assigning weights, what we do is we randomly assign weights. Initially we have input X one, X two, X three. We randomly assign some weight W one, W two, W three, and so on.

Now it's always necessary that whatever weights we assign to our input, those weights are actually correct, meaning that those weights are company significant in predicting your output. So how a multilayer perceptron works is a set of inputs are passed to the first hidden layer. Now the activations from that layer are passed through the next layer.

And from that layer, it's passed to the next hidden layer, until you reach the output layer. From the output layer, you'll form the two classes, class one and class two. Basically, you'll classify your input into one of the two classes. So that's how a multilayer perceptron works.

BACKPROPAGATION

A very important concept the multiple layer percep-tron is back propagation. Now what is back propagation. Back propagation algorithm is a supervised learning method for multilayer perceptron's.

Okay, now why do we need back propagation? So guys, when we are designing a neural network in the beginning, we initialize weights with some random values, or any variable for that fact.

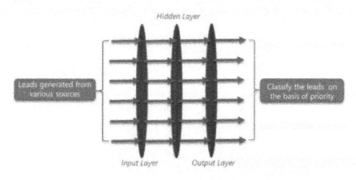

The Backpropagation algorithm is a supervised learning method for Multilayer Perceptron.

Maximum weight is assigned to the most important lead/input.

Now, obviously, we need to make sure that these weights actually are correct, meaning that these weights show the sig-nificance of each predictor variable. These weights have to fit our model in such a way that our output is very precise.

So let's say that we randomly selected some weights in the beginning, but our model output is much more different than our actual output, meaning that our error value is very huge. So how will you reduce this error.

Basically, what you need to do is we need to somehow explain to the model that we need to change the weight in such a way that the error becomes minimum. So the main thing is the weight and your error is very highly related.

The weightage that you give to each input will show how much error is there in your output, because the most significant variables will have the highest weightage. And if the weightage is not correct, then your output is also not correct.

Now, back propagation is a way to update your weights in such a way that your outcome is precise and your error is reduced. So, in short back propagation is used to train a multi-layer perceptron.

It's basically use to update your weights in such a way that your output is more precise, and that your error is reduced. So training a neural network is all about back propagation.

TRAINING A NEURAL NETWORK

So, the most common deep learning algorithm for supervised training of the multilayer perceptron is known as back propagation. So, after calculating the weighted sum of inputs and passing them through the activation function, we propagate backwards and update the weights to reduce the error. It's as simple as that.

TRAINING A NEURAL NETWORK

Now, we will see the error (Absolute and Square)

Input	Desired Output	Model Output (W=3)	Absolute Error	Square Error
0	0	0	0	0
1	2	3	1	1
2	4	6	2	4

So in the beginning, you're going to assign some weights to each of your input. Now these inputs will go through the activation function and it'll go through all the hidden layers and give us an output. Now when you get the output, the output is not very precise, or it is not the desired output. So what you'll do is you'll propagate backwards, and you start updating your weights in such a way that your error is as minimum as possible. So, I'm going to repeat this once more.

So the idea behind back propagation is to choose weights in such a way that your error gets minimized. To understand this, we'll look at a small example. Let's say that we have a data set which has these labels. Okay, your input is zero, one, two, but your desired output is zero, one, and four now the output of your model when W equal to three is like this.

Notice the difference between your model output and your desired output. So, your model output is three, but your desired output is two. Similarly, when your model output is six, your desired output is supposed to be four. Now let's calculate the error when weight is equal to three. The error is zero over here because your desired output is zero, and your model output is also zero. Now the error in the second case is one. Basically, your model output minus your desired output. Three minus two, your error is one. Similarly, your error for the third input is two, which is six minus four. When you take the square, this is actually a very huge difference, your error becomes larger.

Now what we need to do is we need to update the weight value in such a way that our error decreases. Now here we've considered the weight as four. So when you consider the weight as four, your model output becomes zero, four, and eight. Your desired output is zero, two, and four. So your model output becomes zero, four, and eight, which is a lot.

So guys, I hope you all know how to calculate the output over here. What I'm doing is I'm multiplying the input with your weightage. The weightage is four, so zero into four will give me zero. One into four will give me four, and two into four will give me eight. That's how I'm getting my model output over here. For now, this is how I'm getting the output over here.

That's how you calculate your weightage. Now, here, if you see that our desire output is supposed to be zero, two, and four, but we're getting an output of zero, four, and eight. So our error is actually increasing as we increase our weight.

TRAINING A NEURAL NETWORK

Relationship between the assigned weight and the error

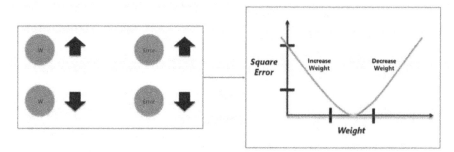

Our error four W equal to four have become zero, four, and 16, whereas the error for W equal to three, zero, one, and four. I mean the square error. So if you look at this, as we increase our weightage, our error is increasing. So, obviously, we know that there is no point in increasing the value of W further.

But if we decrease the value of W, our error actually decreases. Alright, if we give a weightage of two, our error decreases. If we can find a relationship between our weight and error, basically, if you increase the weight, your error also increases.

If you decrease the weight, your error also decreases. Now what we did here is we first initialize some random value to W, and then we propagated forward. Then we notice that there is some error. And to reduce that error, we propagated backwards and increase the value of W.

After that, we notice that the error has increased, and we came to know that we can't increase the w value. Obviously, if your error is increasing with increasing your weight, you will not increase the weight. So again, we propagated backwards, and we decreased the W value.

So, after that, we noticed that the error has reduced. So what we're trying is we're trying to get the value of weight in such a way that the error becomes as minimum as possible so we need to figure out whether we need to increase or decrease the eight value.

Once we know that, we keep on updating the weight value in that direction, until the error becomes minimum. Now you might reach a point where if you further update the weight, the error will again increase. At that point, you need to stop.

Okay, at that point is where your final weight value is there. So, basically, this graph denotes that point. Now this point is nothing but the global loss minimum. If you update the weights further, your error will also increase. Now you need to find out where your global loss minimum is, and that is where your optimum weight lies.

So let me summarize the steps for you. First, you'll calculate the error. This is how far your model output is from your actual output. Then you'll check whether the error is minimized or not. After that, if the error is very huge, then you'll update the weight, and you'll check the error again.

You'll repeat the process until the error becomes minimum now once you reach the global loss minimum, you'll stop updating the weights, and we'll finalize your weight value. This is exactly how back propagation works. Now in order to tell you mathematically what we're doing is we're using a method known as gradient descent.

Okay, this method is used to adjust all the weights in the network with an aim of reducing the error at the output layer. So how gradient descent optimize our works is the first step is you will calculate the error by considering the below equation.

Here you're subtracting the summation of your actual output from your network output. Step two is based on the error you get; you will calculate the rate of change of error with respect to the change in the weight. The learning rate is something that you set in the beginning itself.

Step three is based on this change in weight, you will calculate the new weight. Alright, your updated weight will be your weight plus the rate of change of weight. So, guys, that was all about back propagation and weight update. Now let's look at the limitations of feed forward network. So far, we were discussing the multiple layer perceptron,

LIMITATIONS OF FEED FORWARD NETWORK

The feed forward network. Let's discuss the limitations of these feed forward networks. Now let's consider an example of image classification. Okay, let's say you've trained the neural network to classify images of various animals.

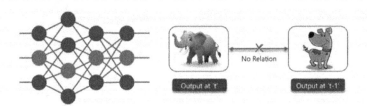

Now let's consider an example. Here the first output is an elephant. We have an elephant. And this output will have nothing to do with the previous output, which is a dog. This means that the output at time T is independent of the output at time T minus one. Now consider this scenario where you will require the use of previously obtained output.

Okay, the concept is very similarly to reading a book. As you turn every page, you need an understanding of the previous pages if you want to make sense of the information, then you need to know what you learned before. That's exactly what you're doing right now. In order to understand deep learning, you have to understand machine learning.

So, basically, with the feed forward network the new output at time T plus one has nothing to do with the output at time T, or T minus one, or T minus two. So feed forward networks cannot be used while predicting a word in a sentence, as it will have absolutely no relationship with the previous set of words.

WHY NOT FEED FORWARD NETWORK?

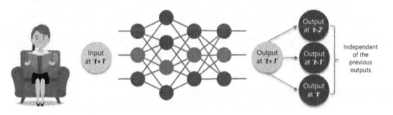

So, a feed forward network cannot be used in use cases wherein you have to predict the outcome based on your previous outcome. So, in a lot of use cases, your previous output will also determine your next output.

So, for such cases, you may not make use of feed forward network. Now, what modification can you make so that your network can learn from your previous mistakes. For this, we have solution.

So, a solution to this is recurrent neural networks. So, basically, let's say you have an input at time T minus one, and you'll get some output when you feed it to the network. Now, some information from this input at T minus one is fed to the next input, which is input at time T. Some information from this output is fed into the next input, which is input at T plus one. So, basically, you keep feeding information from the previous input to the next input. That's how recurrent neural networks really work.

SOLUTION

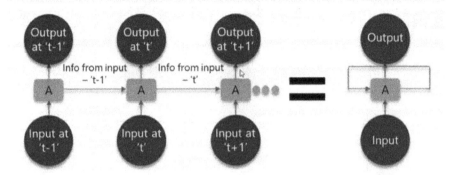

RECURRENT NEURAL NETWORKS

So recurrent networks are a type of artificial neural networks designed to recognize patterns in sequence of data, such as text, genomes, handwriting, spoken words, time series data, sensors, stock markets, and government agencies.

RECURRENT NEURAL NETWORK

Recurrent Networks are a type of artificial neural network designed to recognize patterns in sequences of data, such as text, genomes, handwriting, the spoken word, or numerical times series data emanating from sensors, stock markets and government agencies.

Suppose your gym trainer has made a schedule for you. The exercises are repeated after every third day.

So, guys, recurrent neural networks are actually a very important part of deep learning, because recurring neural networks have applications in a lot of domains. Okay, in time series and in stock markets, the main network that I use are recurrent neural networks, because each of your inputs are correlated now to better understand recurrent neural networks, let's consider a small example let's say that you go to the gym regularly, and the trainer has given you a schedule for your workout.

So basically, the exercises are repeated after every third day. Okay, this is what your schedule looks like. So, make a note that all these exercises are repeated in a proper order or in a sequence every week first, let us use a feedforward network to try and predict the type of exercises that we're going to do. The inputs here are Day of the week, the month, and your health status. Okay, so, neural network has to be trained using these inputs to provide us with the prediction of the exercise that we should do.

Now let's try and understand the same thing using recurrent neural networks. In recurrent neural networks, what we'll do is we'll consider the inputs of the previous day. Okay, so if you did a shoulder workout yesterday, then you can do a bicep exercise today, and this goes on for the rest of the week. However, if you happen to miss a day at the gym, the data from the previously attended time stamps can be considered.

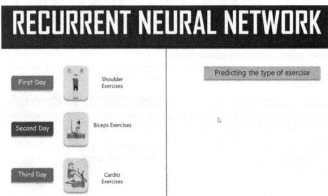

It can be done like this. So, if a model is trained based on the data it can obtain from the previous exercise, the output on the model will be extremely accurate. In such cases, if you need to do know the output at T minus one in order to predict the output at T. In such cases, recurrent neural networks are very essential.

So, basically, I'm feeding some inputs through the neural networks. You'll go through a few functions, and you'll get the output. So, basically, you're predicting the output based on past information or based on your past input. So that's how recurrent neural networks work. Now let's look at another type of neural network known as convolutional neural network.

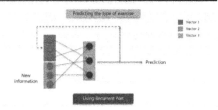

RECURRENT NEURAL NETWORK

Predicting the type of exercise

Vector 1
Vector 2
Vector 3

Prediction

New
Information

Using Recurrent Net

CONVOLUTIONAL NEURAL NETWORKS

To understand why we need convolutional neural networks, let's look at an analogy. How do you think a computer reads an image? Consider this image. This is a New York skyline image. On the first glance, you'll see a lot of buildings and a lot of colours.

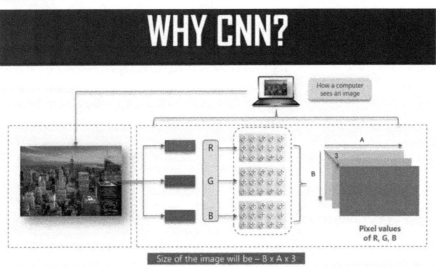

How does a computer process this image? The image is actually broken down into three colour channels, which is the red, green, and blue. It reads in the form of RGB values. Now each of these colour channels are mapped with the image's pixel then the computer will recognize the value associated with each pixel, and determine the size of the image.

Now for the black and white images, there is only one channel, but the concept is still the same. The thing is we cannot make use of fully connected networks when it comes to convolutional neural networks. I'll tell you why. Now consider the first input image.

Okay, first image has size about 28 into 28 into three pixels. And if we input this to a neural network, we'll get about 2,352 weights in the first hidden layer itself. Now consider another example. Okay, let's say we have an image of 200 into 200 into three pixels.

So the size of your first hidden layer becomes around 120,000. Now if this is just the first hidden layer, imagine the number of neurons that you need to process an entire complex image set. This leads to something known as overfitting, because all of the hidden layers are connected.

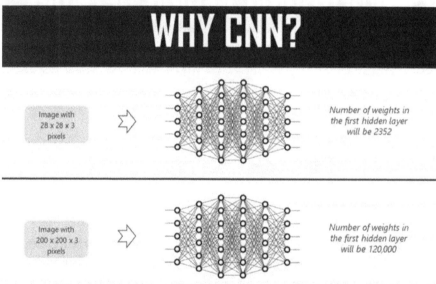

They're massively connected. There's connection between each and every node. Because of this, we face overfitting. We have way too much of data. We have to use way too many neurons, which is not practical. So that's why we have something known as convolutional neural networks. Now convolutional neural networks, like any other neural network are made up of neurons with learnable weights and basis.

So each neuron receives several input. It takes a weighted sum over them, and it gets passed on through some activation function, and finally responds with an output. So, the concept in convolutional neural networks is that the neuron in a particular layer will only be connected to a small region of the layer before it.

Not all the neurons will be connected in a fully-connected manner, which leads to overfitting because we need way too many neurons to solve this problem. Only the regions, which are significant are connected to each other. There is no full connection in convolutional neural networks. So guys, what we did so far is we discussed what a perceptron is.

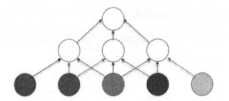

CONVOLUTIONAL NEURAL NETWORKS

In case of CNN the neuron in a layer will only be connected to a small region of the layer before it, instead of all of the neurons in a fully-connected manner.

We discussed the different types of neural networks that are there. We discussed a feedforward neural network. We discuss multi-layer perceptron's we discussed recurrent neural networks, and convolutional neural networks. I'm not going to go too much in depth with these concepts now I'll be executing a demo. If you haven't understood any theoretical concept of deep learning,

please check the given links in the end of the book it will give you a better demo. so that you understand the whole download in a better way. Okay, if you want a more in-depth explanation, I'll leave a couple of links in the end of the book. For now, what I'm gonna do is I'll be running a practical demonstration to show you what exactly download does so, basically, what we're going to do in this demo

DEMO (DEEP LEARNING)

we're going to predict stock prices. Like I said, stock price prediction is one of the very good applications of deep neural networks. You can easily predict the stock price of a particular stock for the next minute or the next day by using deep neural networks.

So that's exactly what we're gonna do in this demo now, before I discuss the code, let me tell you a few things about our data set. The data set contains around 42,000 minutes of data ranging from April to August 2017 on 500 stocks, as well as the total S&P 500 Index price.

So the index and stocks are arranged in a wide format. So, this is my data set, data stocks. It's in the CSV format. So what I'm gonna do is I'm going to use the read CSV function in order to import this data set.

This is just the part of where my data set is stored. This data set was actually cleaned and prepared, meaning that we don't have any missing stock and index prices. So the file does not contain any missing values.

Now what we're gonna do first is we'll drop the data valuable we have a variable known as date, which is not really necessary in predicting our outcome over here. So that's exactly what I'm doing here. I'm just dropping the date variable.

So here, I'm checking the dimensions of the data set. This is pretty understandable, using the shape function to do that. Now, always you make the data as a NumPy array. This makes computation much easier. The next process is the data splicing. I've already discussed data the data splicing with you all. Here we're just preparing the training and the testing data.

So the training data will contain 80% of the total data set. Okay, and also, we are not shuffling the data set. We're just slicing the data set sequentially. That's why we have a test start and the test end variable. In sequence, I'll be selecting the data.

There's no need of shuffling this data set. These are stock prices it does not make sense to shuffle this data. Now in the next step, we're going to do is we're going to scale the data now, scaling data and data normalization is one of the most important steps.

You cannot miss this step I already mentioned earlier what normalization and scaling is. Now most neural networks benefit from scaling inputs. This is because most common activation function of the network's neuron such as tan, hedge, and sigmoid. Tan, hedge, and sigmoid are basically activation functions, and these are defined in the range of minus one to one or zero and one.

So that's why scaling is an important thing in deep neural networks for scaling, again, we'll use the Min Max Scaler. So, we're just importing that function over here. And also, one point to note is that you have to be very cautious about what part of data you're scaling and when you're doing it.

A very common mistake is to scale the whole data set before training and test splits are being applied. So before data splicing itself, you shouldn't be scaling your data. Now this is a mistake because scaling invokes the calculation of statistics.

For example, minimum or maximum range of the variable gets affected. So when performing time series forecasting in real life, you do not have information from future observations at the time of forecasting.

That's why calculation of scaling statistics has to be conducted on training data, and only then it has to be applied to the test data. Otherwise, you're basically using the future information at the time of forecasting, which obviously going to lead to biasness so that's why you need to make sure you do scaling very accurately.

So, basically, what we're doing is the number of features in the training data are stored in a variable known as n stocks. After this, we'll import the infamous TensorFlow. So guys, TensorFlow is actually a very good piece of software and it is currently the leading deep learning and neural network computation framework.

It is based on a C++ low-level backend, but it's usually controlled through Python. So TensorFlow actually operates as a graphical representation of your computations. And this is important because neural networks are actually graphing of data and mathematical operation.

So that's why TensorFlow is just perfect for neural networks and deep learning. So the next thing after importing the TensorFlow library is something known as placeholders. Placeholders are used to store, import, and target data. We need two placeholders in order to fit our model.

So basically, X will contain the network's input, which is the stock prices of all the stocks at time T equal to T. And y will contain the network's output, which is the stock price at time T is equal to T plus one.

Now the shape of the X placeholder means that the inputs are two-dimensional matrix. And the outputs are a one-dimensional vector. So guys, basically, the non-argument indicates that at this point we do not yet know the number of observations that'll flow through the neural network.

We just keep it as a flexible array for now. We'll later define the variable batch size that controls the number of observations in each training batch. Now, apart from this, we also have something know as initializers.

Now, before I tell you what these initializers are, you need to understand that there's something known as variables that are used as flexible containers that are allowed to change during the execution. Weights and bias are represented as variables in order to adapt during training. I already discuss weights and bias with you earlier.

Now weights and bias is something that you need to initialize before you train the model. That's how we discussed it even while I was explaining neural networks to you. So here, basically, we make use of something known as variant scaling initializer and for bias initializer, we make use of zeros initializers.

These are some predefined functions in our TensorFlow model. We'll not get into the depth of those things. Now let's look at our model architecture parameters. So the next thing we have to discuss is the model architecture parameters.

Now the model that we build, it consists of four hidden layers. For the first layer, we've assigned 1,024 neurons which is likely more than double the size of the inputs. The subsequent hidden layers are always half the size of the previous layer, which means that in the hidden layer number two, we'll have 512 neurons. Hidden layer three will have 256. And similarly, hidden layer number four will have 128 neurons.

Now why do we keep reducing the number of neurons as we go through each hidden layer. We do this because the number of neurons for each subsequent layer compresses the information that the network identifies in the previous layer. Of course, there are other possible network architectures that you can apply for this problem statement, but I'm trying to keep it as simple as possible, because I'm introducing deep learning to you all.

So I can't build a model architecture that's very complex and hard to explain. And of course, we have output over here which will be assigned a single neuron. Now it is very important to understand that variable dimensions between your input, hidden, and output layers.

So, as a rule of thumb in multilayer perceptron's, the second dimension of the previous layer is the first dimension in the current layer. So the second dimension in my first hidden layer is going to be my first dimension in my second hidden layer. Now the reason behind this is pretty logical.

It's because the output from the first hidden layer is passed on as an input to the second hidden layer. That's why the second dimension of the previous layer is the same as the first dimension of the next layer or the current layer.

I hope this is understandable. Now coming to the bias dimension over here, the bias dimension is always equal to the second dimension of your current layer, meaning that you're just going to pass the number of neurons in that particular hidden layer as your dimension in your bias. So here, the number of neurons, 1,024, you're passing the same number as a parameter to your bias. Similarly, even for hidden layer number two, if you see a second dimension here is n_neurons_2.

I'm passing the same parameter over here as well. Similarly, for hidden layer three and hidden layer number four. Alright, I hope this is understandable now we come to the output layer. The output layer will obviously have the output from hidden layer number four. This is our output from hidden layer four that's passed as the first dimension in our output layer, and it'll finally have your n target, which is set to one over here. This is our output.

Your bias will basically have the current layer's dimension, which is n target. You're passing that same parameter over here. Now after you define the required weight and the bias variables, the architecture of the network has to be specified. What you do is placeholders and variables need to be combined into a system of sequential matrix multiplication.

So that's exactly what's happening over here. Apart from

this, all the hidden layers need to be transformed by using the activation function. So, activation functions are important components of the network because they introduce non-linearity to the system. This means that high dimensional data can be dealt with the help of the activation functions. Obviously, we have very high dimensional data when it comes to neural networks.

We don't have a single dimension or we don't have two or three inputs. We have thousands and thousands of inputs. So, in order for a neural network to process that much of high dimensional data, we need something known as activation functions.

That's why we make use of activation functions. Now, there are dozens of activation functions, and one of the most common one is the rectified linear unit, rectified linear unit. RELU is nothing but rectified linear unit, which is what we're gonna be using in this model. So, after, you applied the transformation function to your hidden layer, you need to make sure that your output is transposed.

This is followed by a very important function known as cost function. So, the cost function of a network is used to generate a measure of deviation between the network's prediction and the actual observed training targets. So this is basically your actual output minus your model output.

It basically calculates the error between your actual output and your predicted output. So, for regression problems, the mean squared error function is commonly used. I have discussed MSC, mean squared error, before. So, basically, we are just measuring the deviation over here. MSC is nothing bot your deviation from your actual output.

That's exactly what we're doing here. So after you've computed your error, the next step is obviously to update your weight and your bias. So, we have something known as the optimizers. They basically take care of all the necessary computations that are needed to adapt the network's weight and bias variables during the training phase.

That's exactly what's happening over here. Now the main function of this optimizer is that it invokes something known as a gradient. Now if you all remember, we discussed gradient before it basically indicates the direction in which the weights and the bias has to be changed during the training in order to minimize the network's cost function or the network's error.

So, you need to figure out whether you need to increase the weight and the bias in order to decrease the error, or is it the other way around? You need to understand the relationship between your error and your weight variable. That's exactly what the optimizer does. It invokes the gradient. We will give you the direction in which the weights and the bias have to be changed. So now that you know what an optimizer does, in our model, we'll be using something known as the Adam Optimizer.

This is one of the current default optimizers in deep

learning. Adam basically stands for adaptive moment estimation, and it can be considered as a combination between very two popular optimizers called Ad grad and RMSprop. Now let's not get into the depth of the optimizers. The main agenda here is for you to understand the logic behind deep learning. We don't have to go into the functions. I know these are predefined functions which TensorFlow takes care of. Next, we have something known as initializers. Now, initializers are used to initialize the network's variables before training.

We already discussed this before. I'll define the initializer here again. I've already done it earlier in this session. Initializers are already defined. So, I just removed that line of code. Next step would be fitting the neural network. So, after we've defined the place holders, the variables, variables which are basically weights and bias, the initializers, the cost functions, and the optimizers of the network, the model has to be trained.

Now, this is usually done by using the mini batch training method, because we have very huge data set. So, it's always best to use the mini batch training method. Now what happens during mini batch training is random data samples of any batch size are drawn from the training data, and they are fed into the network. So, the training data set gets divided into N divided by your batch size batches that are sequentially fed into the network.

So, one after the other, each of these batches will be fed

into the network. At this point, the placeholder which are your X and Y, they come into play. They store the input and the target data and present them to the network as inputs and targets.

That's the main functionality of placeholders. What they do is they store the input and the target data, and they provide this to the network as inputs and targets. That's exactly what your placeholders do. So, let's say that a sample data batch of X. Now this data batch flows through the network until it reaches the output layer.

There the TensorFlow compares the model's predictions against the actual observed targets, which is stored in Y. If you all remember, we stored our actual observed targets in Y. After this, TensorFlow will conduct something known as optimization step, and it'll update the network's parameters like the weight of the network and the bias.

So after having update your weight and the bias, the next batch is sampled and the process gets repeated. So, this procedure will continue until all the batches have presented to the network. And one full sweep over all batches is known as an epoch. So, I've defined this entire thing over here.

So, we're gonna go through 10 epochs, meaning that all the batches are going to go through training, meaning you're going to input each batch that is X, and it'll flow through the network until it reaches the output layer.

There what happens is TensorFlow will compare your predictions. That is basically what your model predicted against the actual observed targets which is stored in Y. After this, TensorFlow will perform optimization wherein it'll update the network parameters like your weight and your bias. After you update the weight and the bias, the next batch will get sampled and the process will keep repeating.

This happens until all the batches are implemented in the network. So, what I just told you was one epoch. We're going to repeat this 10 times. So, a batch size is 256, meaning that we have 256 batches. So here we're going to assign x and y, what I just spoke to you about. The mini batch training starts over here so, basically, your first batch will start flowing through the network until it reaches the output layer.

After this, TensorFlow will compare your model's prediction. This is where predictions happen. It'll compare your model's prediction to the actual observed targets which is stored in y. Then TensorFlow will start doing optimization, and it'll update the network parameters like your weight and your bias. So, after you update the weight and the biases, the next batch will get input into the network, and this process will keep repeating.

This process will repeat 10 times because we've defined 10 epochs. Now, also during the training, we evaluate the network's prediction on the test set, which is basically the data which we haven't learned, but this data is set aside for every fifth batch, and this is visualized. So, in our problem statement, what a network is going to do is it's going to predict the stock price continuously over a time period of T plus one.

We're feeding it data about a stock price at time T. It's going to give us an output of time T plus one. Now let me run this code and let's see how close our predicted values are to the actual values. We're going to visualize this entire thing, and we've also exported this in order to combine it into a video animation.

I'll show you what the video looks like check that video link in the end of the book suggestions over some screenshots from my computer. So now let's look at our visualization. We'll look at our output. So, the orange basically shows our model's prediction.

So, the model quickly learns the shape and the location of the time series in the test data and showing us an accurate prediction. It's pretty close to the actual prediction. Now as I'm explaining this to you, each batch is running here.

We are at epoch two. We have 10 epochs to go over here. So, you can see that the network is actually adapting to the basic shape of the time series, and it's learning finer patterns in the data. You see it keeps learning patterns and the production is getting closer and closer after every epoch.

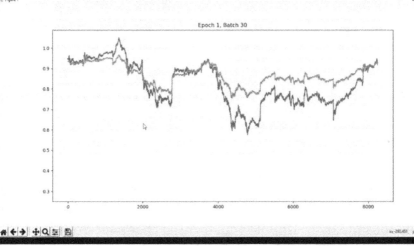

So, let just wait till we reach epoch 10 and we complete the entire process. So, guys, I think the predictions are pretty close, like the pattern and the shape is learned very well by our neural network. It is actually mimicking this network.

The only deviation is in the values. Apart from that, it's learning the shape of the time series data in almost the same way. The shape is exactly the same. It looks very similar to me. Now, also remember that there are a lot of ways of improving your result.

You can change the design of your layers or you can change the number of neurons. You can choose different initialization functions and activation functions. You can introduce something known as dropout layers which basically help you to get rid of overfitting, and there's also something known as early stopping.

Early stopping helps you understand where you must stop your batch training. That's also another method that you can implement for improving your model. Now there are also different types of deep learning model that you can use for this problem.

Here we use the feedforward network, which basically means that the batches will flow from left to right. Okay, so our 10 epochs are over. Now the final thing that's getting calculate is our error, MSC or mean squared error. So, guys, don't worry about this warning. It's just a warning. So, our mean square error comes down to 0.0029 which is pretty low because the target is scaled.

And this means that our accuracy is pretty good. So, guys, like I mentioned, if you want to improve the accuracy of the model, you can use different schemes, you can use different initialization functions, or you can try out different transformation functions. You can use something known as dropout technique and early stopping in order to make the training phase even better.

So, guys, that was the end of our deep learning demo. I hope all of you understood the deep learning demo. For those of you who are just learning deep learning for the first time, it might be a little confusing. So, if you have any doubts regarding the demo, I'll also leave a couple of links in the end of the book, so that you can understand deep learning and demo in a little more depth. Now let's look at our final topic for today,

NATURAL LANGUAGE PROCESSING

which is natural language processing. Now before we understand what text mining is and what natural language processing is, we have to understand the need for text mining and natural language processing.

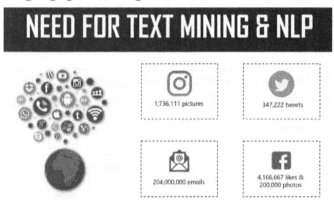

NEED FOR TEXT MINING & NLP

1,736,111 pictures

347,222 tweets

204,000,000 emails

4,166,667 likes & 200,000 photos

So, guys, the number one reason why we need text mining and natural language processing is because of the amount of data that we're generating during this time. Like I mentioned earlier, there are around 2.5 quintillion bytes of data that is created every day, and this number is only going to grow. With the evolution of communication through social media, we generate tons and tons of data. The numbers are on your screen.

These numbers are literally for every minute. On Instagram, every minute, 1.7 million pictures are posted. Okay, 1.7 or more than 1.7 million pictures are posted. Similarly, we have tweets. We have around 347,000 tweets every minute on Twitter. This is actually a lot and lot of data. So, every time we're using a phone, we're generating way too much data. Just watching a video on YouTube is generating a lot of data.

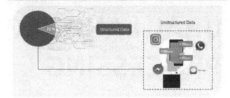

NEED FOR TEXT MINING & NLP

When sending text messages from WhatsApp, that is also generating tons and tons of data. Now the only problem is not our data generation. The problem is that out of all the data that we're generating, only 21% of the data is structured and well-formatted.

The remaining of the data is unstructured, and the major source of unstructured data include text messages from Whats-App, Facebook likes, comments on Instagram, bulk emails that we send out every single day. All of this accounts for the unstructured data that we have today.

Now the question here is what can be done with so much data. Now the data that we generate can be used to grow businesses. By analysing and mining the data, we can add more value to a business. This exactly what text mining is all about.

WHAT IS TEXT MINING?

So, text mining or text analytics is the analysis of data available to us in a day-to-day spoken or written language. It is amazing so much data that we generate can actually be used in text mining. We have data from word documents, PowerPoints, chat messages, emails. All of this is used to add value to a business now the data that we get from sources like social media, IoT, they are mainly unstructured, and unstructured data cannot be used to draw useful insights to grow a business.

WHAT IS TEXT MINING?

Text Mining / Text Analytics is the process of deriving meaningful information from natural language text.

That's exactly why we need to text mining. Text mining or text analytics is the process of deriving meaningful information from natural language text. So, all the data that we generate through text messages, emails, documents, files, are written in natural language text. And we are going to use text mining and natural language processing to draw useful insights or patterns from such data.

Now let's look at a few examples to show you how natural language processing and text mining is used. So now before

I move any further, I want to compare text mining and NLP. A lot of you might be confused about what exactly text mining is and how is it related to natural language processing.

A lot of people have also asked me why is NLP and text mining considered as one and the same and are they the same thing. So, basically, text mining is a vast field that makes use of natural language processing to derive high quality information from the text. So, basically, text mining is a process, and natural language processing is a method used to carry out text mining.

So, in a way, you can say that text mining is a vast field which uses and NLP in order perform text analysis and text mining. So, NLP is a part of text mining. Now let's understand what exactly natural language processing is.

WHAT IS NLP?

Now, natural language processing is a component of text mining which basically helps a machine in reading the text. Obviously, machines don't actually know English or French, they interpret data in the form of zeroes and ones.

So, this is where natural language processing comes in. NLP is what computers and smart phones use to understand our language, both spoken and written language. Now because use language to interact with our device, NLP became an integral part of our life.

NLP uses concepts of computer science and artificial intelligence to study the data and derive useful information from it. Now before we move any further, let's look at a few applications of NLP and text mining.

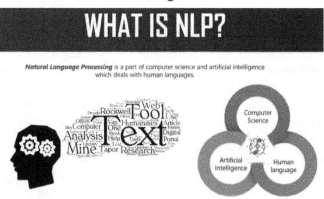

Natural Language Processing is a part of computer science and artificial intelligence which deals with human languages.

APPLICATIONS OF NLP

Now we all spend a lot of time surfing the webs. Have you ever noticed that if you start typing a word on Google, you immediately get suggestions like these?

These features are also known as auto complete. It'll basically suggest the rest of the word for you. And we also have something known as spam detection. Here is an example of how Google recognizes the misspelling Netflix and shows results for keywords that match your misspelling.

APPLICATIONS OF NLP

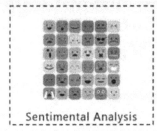

Sentimental Analysis

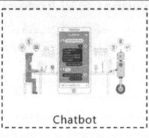

Chatbot

Speech Recognition

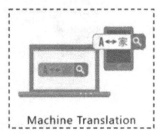

Machine Translation

So, the spam detection is also based on the concepts of text mining and natural language processing. Next, we have predictive typing and spell checkers. Features like auto correct, email classification are all applications of text mining and NLP. Now we look at a couple of more applications of natural language processing.

We have something known as sentimental analysis. Sentimental analysis is extremely useful in social media monitoring, because it allows us to gain an overview of the wider public opinion behind certain topics. So, basically, sentimental analysis is used to understand the public's opinion or customer's opinion on a certain product or on a certain topic.

WHERE IS TEXT MINING USED?

Autocomplete   Spam Detection

Sentimental analysis is actually a very huge part of a lot of social media platforms like Twitter, Facebook. They use sentimental analysis very frequently. Then we have something known as chatbot. Chatbots are basically the solutions for all the consumer frustration, regarding customer call assistance.

So we have companies like Pizza Hut, Uber who have started using chatbots to provide good customer service, apart from that speech recognition. NLP has widely been used in speech recognition. We're all aware of Alexa, Siri, Google Assistant, and Cortana.

WHERE IS TEXT MINING USED?

Predictive typing   Spell checker

These are all applications of natural language processing. Machine translation is another important application of NLP. An example of this is the Google Translator that uses NLP to process and translate one language to the other. Other application includes spell checkers, keywords search, information extraction, and NLP can be used to get useful information from various website, from word documents, from files, and et cetera.

It can also be used in advertisement matching. This basically means a recommendation of ads based on your history. So now that you have a basic understanding of where natural language processing is used and what exactly it is, let's take a look at some important concepts.

TERMINOLOGIES IN NLP

So, firstly, we're gonna discuss tokenization. Now tokenization is the most basic step in text mining. Tokenization basically means breaking down data into smaller chunks or tokens so that they can be easily analysed.

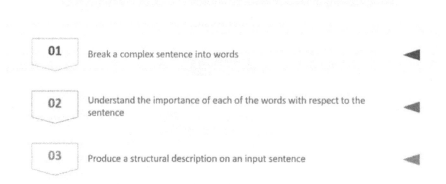

Now how tokenization works is it works by breaking a complex sentence into words. So, you're breaking a huge sentence into words. You'll understand the importance of each of the word with respect to the whole sentence, after which will produce a description on an input sentence.

So, for example, let's say we have this sentence, tokens are simple. If we apply tokenization on this sentence, what we get is this. We're just breaking a sentence into words.

Then we're understanding the importance of each of these words. We'll perform NLP process on each of these words to understand how important each word is in this entire sentence. For me, I think tokens and simple are important words, are is basically another stop word. We'll be discussing about stop words in our further slides.

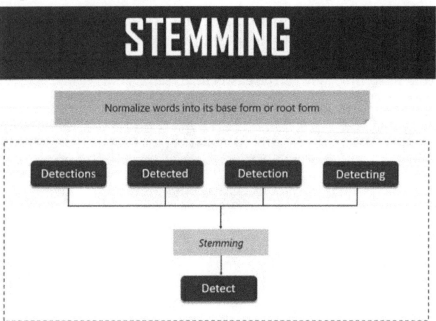

But for now, you need to understand that tokenization is a very simple process that involves breaking sentences into words. Next, we have something known as stemming. Stemming is basically normalizing words into its base form or into its root form.

Take a look at this example. We have words like detection, detecting, detected, and detections. Now we all know that the root word for all these words is detect. Basically, all these words mean detect. So, the stemming algorithm works by cutting off the end or the beginning of the word and taking into account a list of common prefixes and suffixes that can be found on any word.

LEMMITIZATION

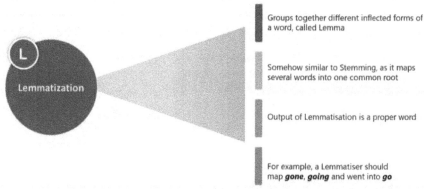

Groups together different inflected forms of a word, called Lemma

Somehow similar to Stemming, as it maps several words into one common root

Output of Lemmatisation is a proper word

For example, a Lemmatiser should map *gone*, *going* and went into *go*

So, guys, stemming can be successful in some cases, but not always. That is why a lot of people affirm that stemming has a lot of limitations. So, in order to overcome the limitations of stemming, we have something known as lemmatization. Now what lemmatization does is it takes into consideration the morphological analysis of the words.

To do so, it is necessary to have a detailed dictionary which the algorithm can look through to link the form back to its lemma. So, basically lemmatization is also quite similar to stemming. It maps different words into one common root. Sometimes what happens in stemming is that most of the words gets cut off. Let's say we wanted to cut detection into detect.

Sometimes it becomes det or it becomes tact, or something like that. So, because of this, the grammar or the importance of the word goes away. You don't know what the words mean anymore. Due to the indiscriminate cutting of the word, sometimes the grammar the understanding of the word is not there anymore.

So that's why lemmatization was introduced. The output of lemmatization is always going to be a proper word. Okay, it's not going to be something that is half cut or anything like that. You're going to understand the morphological analysis and then only you're going to perform lemmatization.

An example of a lemmatize is you're going to convert gone, going, and went into go. All the three words anyway mean the same thing. So, you're going to convert it into go. We are not removing the first and the last part of the word.

STOP WORDS

Are stop words helpful?

What we're doing is we're understanding the grammar behind the word. We're understanding the English or the morphological analysis of the word, and only then we're going to perform lemmatization. That's what lemmatization is all about. Now stop words are basically a set of commonly used words in any language, not just English.

Now the reason why stop words are critical to many applications is that if we remove the words that are very commonly used in a given language, we can finally focus on the important words. For example, in the context of a search engine, let's say you open up Google and you try how to make strawberry milkshake.

What the search engine is going to do is it's going to find a lot more pages that contain the terms how to make, rather than pages which contain the recipe for your strawberry milkshake. That's why you have to disregard these terms.

The search engine can actually focus on the strawberry milkshake recipe, instead of looking for pages that have how to and so on. So that's why you need to remove these stop words. Stop words are how to, begin, gone, various, and, the, all of these are stop words.

They are not necessarily important to understand the importance of the sentence. So, you get rid of these commonly used words, so that you can focus on the actual keywords. Another term you need to understand is document term matrix. A document term matrix is basically a matrix with documents designated by roles and words by columns.

So, if your document one has this sentence, this is fun, or has these word, this is fun, then you're going to get one, one, one over here. In document two, if you see we have this and we have is, but we do not have fun. So that's what a document term matrix is.

It is basically to understand whether your document contains each of these words. It is a frequency matrix. That is what a document term matrix is. Now let's move on and look at a natural language processing demo.

NLP DEMO

So, what we're gonna do is we're gonna perform sentimental analysis. Now like I said, sentimental analysis is one of
the most popular applications of natural language processing. It
refers to the processing of determining whether a given piece of
text or a given sentence of text is positive or negative.

So, in some variations, we consider a sentence to also be
neutral. That's a third option. And this technique is commonly
used to discover how people feel about a particular topic or
what are people's opinion about a particular topic. So, this is
mainly used to analyse the sentiments of users in various forms,
such as in marketing campaigns, in social media, in e-commerce
websites, and so on.

So now we'll be performing sentimental analysis using
Python. So, we are going to perform natural language processing by using the NaiveBayesClassifier. That's why we are importing the NaiveBayesClassifier.

So, guys, Python provides a library known as natural
language toolkit. This library contains all the functions that are
needed to perform natural language processing. Also, in this library, we have a predefined data set called movie reviews. What

we're gonna do is we're going to download that from our NLTK, which is natural language toolkit. We're basically going to run our analysis on this movie review data set. And that's exactly what we're doing over here.

Now what we're doing is we're defining a function in order to extract features. So, this is our function. It's just going to extract all our words. Now that we've extracted the data, we need to train it, so we'll do that by using our movie reviews data set that we just downloaded. We're going to understand the positive words and the negative words. So, what we're doing here is we're just loading our positive and our negative reviews. We're loading both of them.

After that, we'll separate each of these into positive features and negative features. This is pretty understandable. Next, we'll split the data into our training and testing set. Now this is something that we've been doing for all our demos. This is also known as data splicing. We've also set a threshold factor of 0.8 which basically means that 80% of your data set will belong to your training, and 20% will be for your testing.

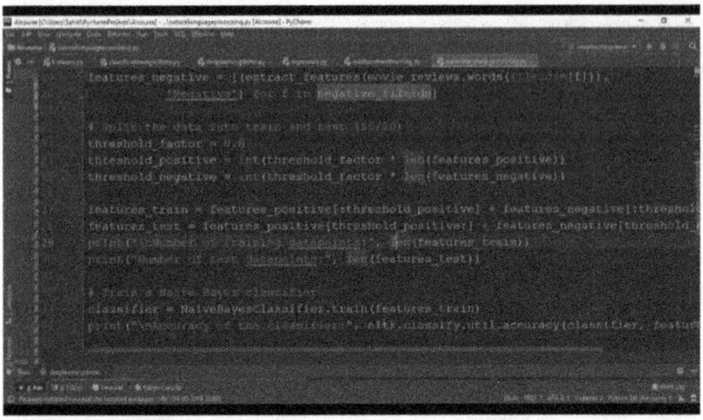

You're going to do this even for your positive and your negative words. After that, you're just extracting the features again, and you're just printing the number of training data points that you have. You're just printing the length of your training features and you're printing the length of your testing features. We can see the output, let's run this program.

So, if you see that we're getting the number of training data points as 1,600 and your number of testing data points are 400, there's an 80 to 20% ration over here. After this, we'll be using the NaiveBayesClassifier and we'll define the object for the NaiveBayesClassifier with basically classifier, and we'll train this using our training data set. We'll also look at the accuracy of our model. The accuracy of our classifier is around 73%, which is a really good number.

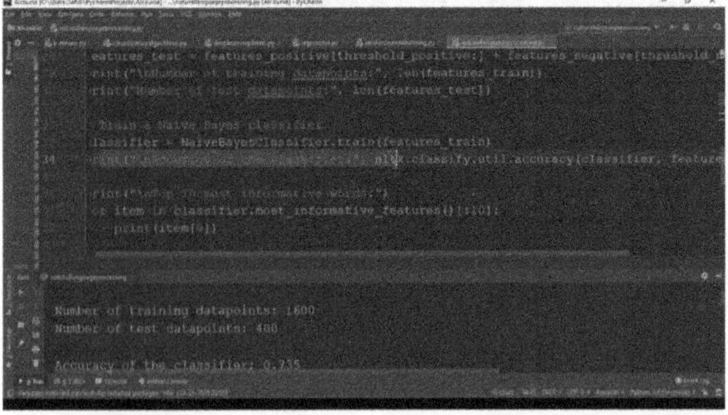

Now this classifier object will actually contain the most informative words that are obtained during analysis. These words are basically essential in understanding which word is classified as positive and which is classified as negative.

What we're doing here is we're going to review movies. We're going to see which movie review is positive or which movie review is negative. Now this classifier will basically have all the informative words that will help us decide which is a positive review or a negative review.

Then we're just printing these 10 most informative words, and we have outstanding, insulting, vulnerable, ludicrous, uninvolving, avoids, fascination, and so on. These are the most important words in our text. Now what we're gonna do is we're gonna test our model. I've randomly given some reviews.

If you want, let's add another review. We'll say I loved the movie. So, I've added another review over here. Here we're just printing the review, and we're checking if this is a positive review or a negative review. Now let's look at our predictions.

We'll save this and... I forgot to put a comma over here. Save it and let's run the file again. So, these were our randomly written movie reviews. The predicted sentiment is positive. Our probability score was 0.61. It's pretty accurate here.

This is a dull movie and I would never recommend it, is a negative sentiment. The cinematography is pretty great, that's a positive review. The movie is pathetic is obviously a negative review. The direction was terrible, and the story was all over the place.

This is also considered as a negative review. Similarly, I love the movie is what I just inputted, and I've got a positive review on that. So our classifier actually works really well. It's giving us good accuracy and it's classifying the sentiments very accurately.

So, guys, this was all about sentimental analysis. Here we basically saw if a movie review was positive or negative.

So guys, that was all for our NLP demo. I hope all of you understood this. It was a simple sentimental analysis that we saw through Python. So again, if you have doubts I'll also leave a couple of links in the end of the book, so that you can understand deeply.

So, guys, that was our last module, which was on natural language processing. Now before I end today's session, I would like to discuss with you the machine learning engineers program that we have.

MACHINE LEARNING MASTER'S PROGRAM

So, we all are aware of the demand of the machine learning engineer. So, at, we have a master's program that involves 200-plus hours of interactive training. So, the machine learning master's program at has around nine modules and 200-plus hours of interactive learning.

So, let me tell you the curriculum that this course provides. So, your first module will basically cover Python programming. It'll have all the basics and all your data visualization, your GUI programming, your functions, and your object-oriented concepts.

The second module will cover machine learning with Python. So, you'll supervise algorithms and unsupervised algorithms along with statistics and time series in Python will be covered in your second module. Your third module will have graphical modelling.

This is quite important when comes to machine learning. Here you'll be taught about decision making, graph theory, inference, and Bayesian and Markov's network, and module number four will cover reinforcement learning in depth.

Here you'll understanding dynamic programming, temporal difference, Bellman equations, all the concepts of reinforcement learning in depth. All the detail in advance concepts of reinforcement learning. So, module number five will cover NLP with Python.

You'll understand tokenization, stemming lemmatization, syntax, tree parsing, and so on. And module number six will have module six will have artificial intelligence and deep learning with TensorFlow. This module is a very advanced version of all your machine learning and reinforcement learning that you'll learn.

Deep learning will be in depth over here. You'll be using TensorFlow throughout. They'll cover all the concepts that we saw, CNN, RNN. it'll cover the various type of neural networks, like convolutional neural networks, recurrent neural networks, long, short-term memory, neural networks, and auto encoders and so on.

The seventh module is all about PySpark. It'll show you how Spark SQL works and all the features and functions of Spark ML library. And the last module will finally cover about Python Spark using PySpark. Appropriate from these seven modules, you'll also get two free self-paced courses. Let's actually take a look at the course. So, this is your machine learning engineer master's program. You'll have nine courses, 200-plus hours of interactive learning.

This is the whole course curriculum, which we just discussed. Here there are seven modules. Apart from these seven modules, you'll be given two free self-paced courses, which I'll discuss shortly. You can also get to know the average annual salary for a machine learning engineer, which is over $134,000. And there are also a lot of job openings in the field of machine learning AI and data science.

So the job titles that you might get are machine learning engineer, AI engineer, data scientist, data and analytics manger, NLP engineer, and data engineer. So, this is basically the curriculum. Your first will by Python programming certification, machine learning certification using Python, graphical modelling, reinforcement learning, natural language processing, AI and deep learning with TensorFlow.

Python Spark certification training using PySpark. If you want to learn more about each of these modules, you can just go and view the curriculum. They'll explain each and every concept that they'll be showing in this module. All of this is going to be covered here.

This is just the first module. Now at the end of this project, you will be given a verified certificate of completion with your name on it, and these are the free elective courses that you're going to get. One is your Python scripting certification training. And the other is your Python Statistics for Data Science Course.

Both of these courses explain Python in depth. The second course on statistics will explain all the concepts of statistics probability, descriptive statistics, inferential statistics, time series, testing data, data clustering, regression modelling, and so on.

So, each of the module is designed in such a way that you'll have a practical demo or a practical implementation after each and every model. So all the concept that I theoretically taught to you will be explained through practical demos. This way you'll get a good understanding of the entire machine learning and AI concepts.

So, if any of you are interested in enrolling for this program or if you want to learn more about the machine learning course offered by, please check the link in the end of the book, and we'll get back to you with all the details of the course. So, guys, with this, we come to the end of this AI full course session. I hope all of you have understood the basic concepts and the idea behind AI machine learning, deep learning, and natural language processing.

So, if you still have doubts regarding any of these topics, Ill clarity for you better you will watch that videos that links on next page, and I'll try to answer all your queries. So, guys, thank you so much for purchase the book. Have a great day. I hope you have enjoyed this book. Please be kind enough to review it. Happy learning.

USEFUL LINKS: -

Artificial Intelligence Tutorial -
https://youtu.be/JMUxmLyrhSk
Python Course   -
https://www.youtube.com/watch?v=vaysJAMDaZw
Statistics and Probability Tutorial -
https://www.youtube.com/watch?v=XcLO4f1i4Yo
Check out the entire Machine Learning Playlist here -
https://bit.ly/2NG9tK4

Finally thanks to Edureka !

www.ingramcontent.com/pod-product-compliance
Lightning Source LLC
LaVergne TN
LVHW041209050326
832903LV00021B/539